A LOYAL FOE

by
Ivy Bolton

Originally Published in 1933
Cover illustration by Tina DeKam
Cover design by Tina DeKam
© 2021 Jenny Phillips
goodandbeautiful.com

Table of Contents

Historical Note

MISS BOLTON has chosen for the setting of her story a period of English history made familiar to many by Shakespeare. Writing in Queen Elizabeth's reign, when the struggle between the houses of Lancaster and York had become past history, Shakespeare found in the career of Richard III, the last of the Yorkist kings, a theme admirably suited for a great tragic drama. That he looked upon Richard with prejudiced eyes cannot be denied. Queen Elizabeth's grandfather, Henry Tudor, had won the crown by overthrowing Richard in the battle of Bosworth, and the chroniclers from whose narratives Shakespeare drew his material thought to enhance Henry VII's renown by emphasizing the sins of the king he had defeated and killed. But though efforts have been made to prove that Richard was not the coldblooded villain Shakespeare represents, they have accomplished little or nothing. Shakespeare's Richard remains substantially the Richard of history.

When Rex Damory was born, Richard's brother, Edward IV

occupied the throne. Edward, too, won the crown with his sword. The battle of Towton made him, in 1461, master of England and left his predecessor, the Lancastrian Henry VI, a wandering fugitive in the country over which he had ruled for nearly forty years. But the first ten years of Edward's reign were full of troubles, arising in part from the conditions left by years of civil war, and in part from the jealousy and ambition of the great earl who had helped him to win the crown, Warwick, the king-maker. Choosing a wife to please himself, Edward married in secret the beautiful Elizabeth Woodville, the widow of a man who had fallen in the cause of Henry VI, and Warwick, who had been in negotiation for a royal bride for his young master, never forgave the king for deceiving him. From that day there was a bitter feud between Warwick and the queen's relatives, the Woodvilles, upon whom Edward unwisely bestowed many favors. The final result was a renewal of the Wars of the Roses, the replacing of Henry VI upon the throne by Warwick, and the flight of Edward to the court of his brother-in-law, the Duke of Burgundy. In the spring of 1471, however, Edward returned and, after winning two great battles at Barnet and Tewkesbury, in which Warwick and also Henry VI's only son perished, imprisoned Henry in the Tower of London and again assumed the crown.

From the time of Edward's second winning of the crown until his death twelve years later, there was no more civil war in England. But quarrelling and plotting still went on at the royal court. Edward never again leaned on any man as he had leaned on Warwick. At great cost he had learned the folly of permitting any subject to exert such power as Warwick had had, and he did not repeat his mistake. If he can be said to have had any favorite in his later years, that favorite was the younger of his two brothers, Richard, Duke of Gloucester.

Richard, like Edward, had remarkable military genius, and

that may have increased Edward's affection for him. In addition, Richard never gave Edward cause to doubt his loyalty, and this was the more appreciated by the king because his other brother, the Duke of Clarence, proved a traitor. When, after a form of trial, Clarence was condemned for his sins and put to death in the Tower, rumor, which already blamed Gloucester for the killing of Henry VI's son at the battle of Tewkesbury and for the mysterious death of Henry himself in the Tower soon after that battle, declared that he knew too much about Clarence's death. But men were used to murder in those days. Moreover, Richard's hands were blood-stained on his behalf. That Richard was trying to clear his own road to the throne was an idea which, I am inclined to believe, never entered Edward's mind, although Miss Bolton apparently thinks that Edward did harbor such a suspicion. There is room for difference of opinion, as we cannot know certainly the secret workings of any man's mind.

On the whole, Edward's subjects were contented in the last years of his reign. London was already a great city, and, in many other towns as well, workers were busy, merchants were piling up fortunes, and life was pleasant. From the seaports of the kingdom, ships were carrying away vast quantities of English wool, the finest wool to be found in Europe, and large cargoes of English cloth. To the same seaports, other ships were bringing tuns upon tuns of the wine so freely drunk in those days, and innumerable manufactured articles that English people wanted but did not produce. Thus England was daily growing in wealth. She was also daily growing fonder of wealth and, consequently, of the peace necessary to the increase of wealth. Edward, who himself made money by exporting wool and cloth, had given her that peace, and in gratitude she was ready to overlook his faults, though they were not few.

Unfortunately dynastic quarrels seem to have as many lives as a cat. They go on living long after they ought, logically, to be dead. Over in Brittany there was a youth who, though he had fled penniless from England after the battle of Tewkesbury, had carried with him something more precious than gold, namely, his title to the English crown. Henry Tudor, Earl of Richmond, had become, through the death of Henry VI and his son, the head of the house of Lancaster, and those Englishmen whose hearts had clung to Henry VI as long as he lived, had now transferred their loyalty to Henry's youthful namesake.

That Henry Tudor was a danger to his throne Edward was so well aware that he tried time and again to secure his surrender by the Duke of Brittany. All such efforts failed, however, and Richmond was still across the Channel when, in April 1483, Edward died. A few months later, Gloucester seized the throne and Edward's two young sons died in the Tower as mysteriously as Henry VI had died there.

Now came the great opportunity of those who had never willingly submitted to the house of York. Gloucester had gone too far. The murder of the little princes, the story of which Miss Bolton tells in such a touching way, was a crime too barbarous to be endured, for it outraged not only the strong sense of justice and right so characteristic of Englishmen, but also their affection for children. Vengeance was not secured immediately. Richmond's first attempt to invade England failed because Richard was forewarned and because a storm scattered the earl's ships, but when the earl came a second time, the country rose to welcome him. Richard fell in the battle of Bosworth fighting as bravely as any man could, but no one shed any tears for him when his naked body, thrown carelessly across the back of a horse, was carried to Leicester and buried in the church of the Grey Friars. He had disgraced both himself and the throne he had stolen. He had also destroyed the peace which England had so long desired and thought she had at last obtained. Henry Tudor restored that peace, and under the Tudor dynasty England was destined to rise to a greatness she had never before known.

This, briefly, is the historical background of A *Loyal Foe*. Miss Bolton's sympathetic imagination has added details, and the story she has written is so vivid that I think the boys and girls who read it will feel that they, like Rex Damory, have lived in the stirring days of the Wars of the Roses.

〜 Cora L. Scofield 〜

List of Main Characters

Rex Damory—main character, Red Rose/Lancaster supporter, becomes companion of Prince Edward

Hugh Damory—Rex's father, Red Rose/Lancaster supporter

Rance—squire to Damory family

Nicholas Leslie—brother to Elsie Leslie, Hugh's wife and Rex's mother; enemy to the Damory family

Ruth Damory—Rex's twin sister; kidnapped as a child by Nicholas Leslie

King Edward—Current king of England; also known historically as Edward IV; son of Richard, Duke of York, who led the York rebellion to begin the Wars of the Roses

Lady Queen Elizabeth—wife of King Edward; widow of a Red Rose knight

Richard, Duke of Gloucester—King Edward's brother

Thomas, Lord Woodville—relative to the queen

John Fortescue—friend and ally of Damory family; Lancaster supporter

Princess Elizabeth—oldest daughter of King Edward; marries Henry Tudor

Prince Edward—oldest son of King Edward

Ruth Leslie—maiden to Princess Elizabeth, relative of Nicholas Leslie

Joyce Deventry—maiden to Princess Elizabeth

Nurse Gillian—nurse to King Edward's children, former nurse to Elsie Leslie (Rex's mother)

Forrest, FitzAllen, and Thorsby—men loyal to Nicholas Leslie

Henry Tudor—nephew to King Henry VI of Lancaster; becomes king of England and marries Princess Elizabeth (also known as Henry of Richmond)

Father Oswald—Augustinian prior who is loyal to the Damory family

I

Damory's Woe

I, HUGO De Damory, do erect this shrine to the memory of John, the wise man, whom I, in my sin, sent to the stake, stealing his land for my Tower, for which he vowed I and all my line would be punished. Ye who shelter here, pray for my sinful soul.

> *For the wrong so foully done,*
> *Damory's lord must aye atone,*
> *Till maiden's hand bring harmony*
> *And joy and peace to Damory*
> *And Damory's lord in bitter woe*
> *Conquer Damory's fiercest foe.*

THE WORDS were carved beneath the shrine, and Rex Damory read them aloud as he stood there one bright May morning, waiting for his father. Built into the tower itself, the shrine was of great beauty. The hand which had

1

carved the Divine Face had been that of a lover as well as an
artist. Rumor said that old Sir Hugo, seeking a worker in stone
for his shrine, had found one in a small, forgotten monastery,
where an old monk's skill in sculpture had kept pace with a life
of prayer and devotion to his Lord. Rex bent his knee and murmured a prayer as was his custom, for since his babyhood, this
shrine had been a favorite place of his, and old Sir Hugo in his
stormy penitence had always held his interest.

"I wish that I could raise the punishment," he mused aloud
as he seated himself on the narrow stone seat. "There needeth
joy for Damory, though Father and I be comrades, true and
staunch, and though he says that I be his comfort. But his eyes
are always sad, and it is not only for the loss of my sweet mother.
There is something else besides. Who is Damory's fiercest foe? I
wonder where he may be."

He clasped his hands about his knee as he surveyed his home
with loving eyes, the keep and battlements of Norman days,
supplemented by many a rambling wing and turret of Later
England. Southward lay the town of Blandford and on the other
three sides was the broad sweep of Dorset Down, broken by
copse and woodland and the winding Roman road to the sea. It
was a fair place, but old Damory Court bore not only the scars
of old-time warfare, but the more recent marks of the Wars of
the Roses. Rex, only son of the present Sir Hugh, could not remember the two assaults on Damory in his babyhood when, just
before Tewkesbury, the White Rose held the place for four days.
It had been recaptured by its lord, but it was a dearly bought
victory, for the Lady of Damory had fallen in the strife, flinging herself between her husband and his opponent's blow. Sir
Hugh's hair had whitened in that night and, after the Red Rose
defeat, he had come back, a silent and sorrow-stricken man, to
care for his little son. Between Rex and his father as the years
went on there grew up a love and devotion unusual in those

2

formal days.

"Where can I find Sir Hugh Damory, young sir?"

The boy rose to his feet as a young man accosted him. "He is in the house. Can I serve you in aught? I am his son."

"My message is to him alone." The messenger threw back his cloak revealing a Red Rose badge, and Rex at once summoned old Rance, the squire, who had been standing with the horses in readiness for the daily ride.

"Take this messenger to my father, Rance," Rex said, and stood watching them as they crossed the greensward below the moat and mounted the drawbridge.

I wonder if the Red Rose is in the field again, the boy thought; then he started as a stern and authoritative voice spoke behind him.

"What did yon stranger want and whence came he?"

The speaker had ridden up over the soft turf behind the boy. He had dismounted and held his bridle rein. He was richly dressed, with a heavy riding cloak of miniver over a knight's armor, though his hands were covered by heavy leather riding gloves, and his helm hung at his saddlebow. He wore a furred velvet cap on hair slightly gray. He was tall and gave an appearance of strength, but his face held no charm. Thick brows over small pale eyes and a mouth set in cruel curves gave indication of a stern, unyielding man.

"Who was yon messenger and whence did he come?" he repeated.

"By what right do you ask, sir?" Rex returned.

"I want an answer to my question."

Rex did not give way. "You are on private grounds, sir. Why do you trespass on the lands of Damory and ask questions concerning my father's business?"

"Your father is a Red Rose rebel, and I am an accredited messenger of the King. So you are Rex Damory! An answer at once."

"I have none for you, sir. The man told me nothing of his business nor whence he came. Had he done so it is no right of mine to repeat it. If you desire further information, you must go to my father himself."

The man laughed harshly. "Troth, but that would be a putting of my head in the lion's mouth! Have you never heard of Nicholas Leslie?"

"I have not. My mother was a Leslie. Are you kin to her?"

"I am, though that matters not at present. My business is to find out how Damory stands. It is a serious thing to refuse the King's behest, boy."

"Of which you bring no proof."

"Do you give me the lie?"

Rex bowed. "I do not, sir. But you are asking questions concerning my father's guest. It is not my place to answer in any case, and certainly not to give information to one who seems to consider himself Damory's foe."

"You will find me yours, if you are not careful, Rex Damory. I am no mean opponent, I warn you. Remember your sister Ruth!"

"My sister? I never had one to my knowledge. If I had, she must be dead."

"What would Hugh Damory give to know the truth concerning her I wonder? But he never will. She is dead to him at any rate. So Hugh has kept you in ignorance! It is like him. Well, no matter. Are you going to answer my questions or take the consequences?"

"I will take the consequences, Sir Nicholas. You had best not handle that dagger. I have men-at-arms within call."

He beckoned to an undergroom, but old Rance was back at his post and came towards them with swift steps. He saluted Rex.

"What is it, my young lord?"

4

"This gentleman would threaten me, Rance. He desires to know the business of the young man who sought my father a few minutes ago, and I have no answer for him. He gives no definite reason for asking, save that he is an accredited messenger of the King and that his name is Nicholas Leslie."

Into the old squire's face flashed a look of blackest hate. His hand clenched on his sword. For a moment he seemed unable to speak but he regained his self-control, though his words were grimly stern. "You have dared to come hither, Sir Nicholas Leslie? Have you not wrought ill enough to this house without showing your evil face here again?"

Nicholas Leslie laughed in mockery. "Look to your nursling, Rance the squire. The punishment of Damory still holds good." He pointed to the inscription on the shrine. "*Damory's fiercest foe* still lives and does not forget. Till my life's end will Damory lie beneath my hate. The hour is striking for your rebel lord, but this lad has still to face me. Moreover, have a care to yourself. It is well known that you followed your lord to the wars, and we may hang you yet."

The veins stood out on Rance's forehead. He half drew his sword. "Only Sir Hugh's own command is your safety, Sir Nicholas Leslie. I have never yet disobeyed his behest, and I shall not now. But there are others within call who also remember our sweet lady and your foul blow. They will be less obedient. Get you gone, for in five minutes I shall summon them."

Sir Nicholas shrank back at his words, then with a contemptuous sneer he remounted his horse. "We shall meet again, Rex Damory. Beware that house. And you, too, will find that I have not forgotten, Rance. Look to yourself! This is an ill day's work for you both."

He set spurs to his horse and galloped away. Rex turned to the squire.

"What does it all mean, Rance?"

5

The squire shook his head. "It means enough to make me uneasy, my young lord. A heavier punishment to Damory hath Nicholas Leslie been than old Sir Hugo and all his sin. I fear for my lord, and I wish that you had been elsewhere today. Your father would be safer in France, methinks."

"Why do you sentence me to exile, old friend?" asked a clear voice behind them, and the two turned to face Sir Hugh Damory. He was a man older than his years, but in spite of his silver hair, there was still much of his youthful strengths and comeliness, and it was small wonder that his presence brought a look of love and admiration to the eyes of his young son. He laid his hand on Rex's shoulder.

"What has happened to alarm you, Rance?"

The squire pointed to the disappearing horseman. "Yonder rides Sir Nicholas Leslie, my lord. Methought he was content with the evil which he had wrought, but it seems that he still plots mischief. It would seem true that a Torsman with a blood feud never forgets. He was questioning my young lord here about the messenger who has just come to you."

"I trust you told him naught, Rex."

"I did not, my Father. He was sorely angered and rode off vowing vengeance on us all."

"I would that he had questioned someone else. He is ill to cross. Rance, will you gather a dozen men-at-arms for me? I want tried men who can keep their own counsel. You must stay here to guard Rex, and I will take Roger with me. The message which has come bids me ride forth to consult with Lord Medanham, Sir Harry Dalton, Lord Forthingay, and other Red Rose leaders."

The old squire looked troubled. "Is such an expedition wise, Sir Hugh?"

"It is not a question for wisdom, old friend. Our young Prince, Henry of Richmond, is in danger. Through him the Red Rose has called, and a Red Rose man can only obey. Though Ed-

6

ward of York seems secure upon his throne, his health is failing, and his heir is a lad some years younger than Rex. We must be ready to act quickly."

"I see," the old man agreed reluctantly. "Must I bide here, my lord?"

"You must. In the face of this new interest of Sir Nicholas', I dare not leave Rex undefended. He may try the old plan again, and I must have someone here that I can trust. We go to no battle unless our conference has been betrayed, and I scarce see how that can be. Roger is a trusty squire, Rance."

Rance bowed in submission and turned away. Sir Hugh seated himself on the low seat beneath the shrine.

"Sit down, Rex. We cannot ride today, and I know you are full of questions. Ask them, lad."

"I found out that Nicholas Leslie is your foe, Father. He spoke, too, of my sister, Ruth. What did he mean? I knew not that I had a sister."

"You do not remember her at all?"

Rex searched his memory. "I have a kind of dim memory of a little maid who played with me and of one, who I think must have been my mother, teaching me the old rhyme yonder, kissing me and telling me that I must lift the punishment."

"Aye. Elsie always prayed for that, and the two of you prattled the old rhyme before I thought you could lisp the words. Your remembrance is correct, boy. The little maid was your twin sister, Ruth. Did Nicholas Leslie speak of her as alive or dead, Rex?" There was a world of wistful longing in Sir Hugh's voice as he asked the question.

"He said that you would give much to know but that you never would. Will you tell me the whole tale, Father, if it be not too hard a one for you?"

Sir Hugh was silent for some moments and Rex, looking at him, saw that his eyes were filled with tears. He leaned lovingly against him and Sir Hugh drew him closer.

"My little maid! God keep her! Aye, Rex, you shall hear the tale. It is full time that you should know it, and it has been in my mind to tell you for many months now. Like Rance, I had hope that Nicholas Leslie had satisfied his vengeance for a mere boyish quarrel. But a Torsman—for he comes of an old Devonshire family—does not easily forget a wrong, and Nicholas is ill to cross.

"This trouble of the rival Roses was at the bottom of our own, and I was a boy still in my teens, when with Nicholas Leslie, my fellow page, I went in Lord Erskine's train to London. We had never been friends, but my lord kept stern rule, and even my hot temper was perforce held in check till our elders became involved in strife. The political feeling was running high, for King Henry's health had failed; Queen Margaret was unpopular and Warwick, the King-maker as they called him later, had thrown all his great influence on the side of Richard, Duke of York. It was for the Regency that the fight began, but one day as we all walked in the palace rose garden, Lord Warwick said openly that Richard was our rightful King. The Duke of Somerset took the matter up, and the two great lords wrangled hotly. As we drew near, Lord Warwick gathered a white rose and set it in his cap.

"'By my great name, when this shall blush as red as yonder crimson blossom, then will I acknowledge the claim of Harry of Lancaster,' he said. Lord Somerset snatched the red rose.

"'By bright Saint George, but this will have to match the snow before I acknowledge your upstart traitor as king or regent and so desert mine own liege lord,' he cried; and instantly, the attending nobles and their followers began to pluck the roses red and white. As I fastened my crimson bud, Nicholas Leslie drawled an insult at the King.

"'A half French madman has no claim to loyalty,' he said. 'No crimson rose for me.'

"The hot blood rushed to my face. 'You speak of your liege lord,' I told him. 'Be silent, traitor.'

"He drew his dagger, and I came nigh to paying for that taunt with my life. Lord Erskine interposed, and at the investigation which followed, my fellow pages told of Nicholas Leslie's words. Lord Erskine dismissed him from the household, and Nicholas departed, vowing vengeance and a blood feud on me. But I soon forgot him, and he never crossed my path again until after I had wooed and won sweet Elsie Leslie, the fairest maid in Devonshire, aye, and in England, too. Our wedding morn dawned bright and gladsome, save only for the clouds of wartime and the dangers which beset us all. There was a large gathering of her kinsfolk—I had none, being an only son—and suddenly, I saw him. Elsie called him forward.

"'My kinsman, Nicholas Leslie,' she said.

"I held out my hand, but he refused it. 'I have met Hugh Damory before,' he answered curtly, and Elsie looked puzzled. 'Though you wed a thousand times with the Leslies, our score is still unsettled. My day cometh.'

"I laughed and he turned away. I saw the terror in Elsie's eyes, and then my anger rose against him for clouding her marriage morn. Still, I was not alarmed, though I had ever heard ill of the hate of Torsman, and we were on opposite sides. In my great happiness, I cast care to the winds. I never gave him a thought.

"Duty took me to the battlefield, but in the pauses of warfare, I tasted joy that is not often granted to a man. You and your sister, Ruth, were born and all seemed well, till five years later when a messenger sought me to tell me that my wife, my children, and my manor of Damory, were in the hands of the White Rose leader, Sir Nicholas Leslie.

"'My lady begs you to hasten,' the messenger ended. 'Sir Nicholas has threatened her safety and the children's as well.'

"How I reached Damory I hardly know. I rode day and night

and surpassed all former feats when we reached home at last. What wonder when I fought for my sweet wife? I took the foe by surprise, and Damory fell at the third assault. Nicholas and I fought hand to hand in the great hall. My sword turned as he lunged, and Elsie threw herself between, receiving the blow meant for my heart. He turned and fled as she fell, while I knelt beside her, half crazed. She was conscious, and in spite of her mortal pain, she read my vengeance in my eyes.

"'Fight him not for me, Hugh,' she whispered. '*Damory's lord in bitter woe conquers Damory's fiercest foe.*'

"I held her close, and even then the last blow fell. The nurse came flying in wild with fear. Nicholas Leslie had sought the nursery, snatched Ruth from her crib and fled with her, thinking no doubt that he held you. Fortunately Elsie did not seem to comprehend, even when I held you for her last kiss. She died in the dawning and, as I sat beside her, I realized that even had her last wish not been my law, the miscreant had tied my hands, for I could neither pursue nor take vengeance, for fear of harm befalling my little maid."

"And our hands are tied still?" Rex's face had flushed in anger. "Would that I had held him and forced the truth from his false lips."

"False lips they are, my son. Steady, Rex." Sir Hugh's touch on his shoulder calmed the angry lad. "Your mother was right. This wrong cannot be righted by bloodshed. Even were he hopelessly cornered, Nicholas Leslie would die, methinks, rather than tell me true. Hate engenders hate, and to stain our own honor will not wipe out past sin. Even if I had seen him, I should have had to let him go. Remembering always, our King and our Cause claim us, but not our own wrongs."

Rex bit his lip. He steadied his voice with an effort.

"I will not rage, Father. But it is hard to be patient under this. Have you never heard aught of Ruth since?"

"He has hidden her securely. As a Red Rose rebel in a White Rose realm, I have been at a disadvantage, all the more since the Leslies are Yorkists. I do not think that she is dead. Nicholas, in his mad vengeance, would not have forborne to send me some inkling of her fate. I think she is hidden among the Leslies. My hope is that you may find her. But today has brought grave danger upon us both. You must face this issue, for even if I return in safety from this expedition for the Red Rose, it will mean exile in Europe for me. Nay, my son, no tears. A soldier and a soldier's son must face peril unflinchingly. Through all these years, the Red Rose has found a refuge in France. But the King and the King's brother, Richard of Gloucester, realize that just there lies the weakness of their rule. An effort is being made to expel us thence, and an appeal has been made to the Duke of Brittany to give up to England young Henry Richmond, the last of Lancaster's line. He is held in half captivity, but his friends believe that his escape could be arranged, if a refuge can be found for him here. His friend, Sir John Fortescue, a Red Rose man, and held as dangerous as our Prince himself, for there is a heavy price upon his head, has come to me to ask me to seek out such Red Rose lords as remain in England and arrange for a refuge, if his escape is compassed, for an open rebellion. This last seems to me to be rank folly, and I shall use all influence against it. But the Prince's safety may depend upon me. I must hasten, for Nicholas Leslie is hard upon the trail."

"May I not go too? I am tall and strong and able to bear a man's part in the fray, Father."

"It is better not. I think there will be no fight. I must have someone here that I can trust, to whom Lord Fortescue may return if aught fall amiss. Will you keep trust?"

"Faithfully, Father."

"There is one thing more, Rex. Mayhap I shall come back to you in safety; mayhap I shall have to give my life for the Cause.

11

Remember if that be so, I lay it down right willingly. If I do not come back, you will be alone and though the days may seem drear and dark to you, keep faith and courage as Damory has ever done. You may be taken to court and there have reason to rue the day when Nicholas Leslie crossed my path and yours. He is high in favor there, the bosom friend of the King's broth-er, the Duke of Gloucester. No one finds life easy there, for the court is at variance, the Queen's party antagonistic to the Duke's. I do not know what Nicholas Leslie may do, but I am certain he will strike at your weakest point. Do not fight him, Rex. Curb that quick temper of yours. A lad of sixteen cannot aid the Cause by weapons. If honor is at stake, oppose him, even though it may mean a scaffold. Bear minor wrongs in silence."

"You ask a hard thing of me, Father. Silence under wrongs is not my wont."

"Nevertheless, it is my charge to you, Rex. An unknown fu-ture is before you. It may be that, lad as you are, you will have to face death, perhaps even endure it."

The boy's face grew grave under the solemn words. "I see that I have to change, Father. Pray God to give me strength."

"He will not forsake you. Remember death, if needs be, for the King, for Cause and honor; but only silence for private wrongs. I trust you, Rex."

He rose and caught the boy in swift embrace. Then, without another word, he summoned Rance and, an hour later, they were ready to start. As the men at arms waited, Sir Hugh drew Rex into a little antechamber. There stood the messenger of the morn.

"Sir John, this is my son," Sir Hugh said. "I wanted him to see you so that he might recognize you at need."

The young man smiled. Rex looked into a strong face with resolute mouth, fearless eyes, and dauntless bearing. John Forte-scue took the boy's hand.

"I trust that I shall not have to call upon you, Rex Damory. I pray likewise that no harm may come to your brave father by this behest. May we meet in happier days by the side of our young Prince."

A few moments later they had mounted and gone, and Rex turned to see old Rance watching them with wistful eyes. It was the first time that he had not ridden behind his lord since Sir Hugh's knighting, and the boy knew what the squire's grief was.

"My father says that we are serving too, Rance," he comforted him. "You must help me, for you see today I have found *Damory's fiercest foe.*"

"God protect you from him," Rance answered. "I would that he had not seen you, my young lord."

THE DAYS of watching passed slowly, and when the fifth one dawned, misgiving came to the brave hearts of the watchers. At noontide, Rance sought Rex.

"I fear there are ill tidings, Lord Rex," he said. "Lord Fortescue, who went forth with Sir Hugh, is returning alone."

The boy's face went white. "Go, meet him and bring him hither, Rance. Then go forth and discover if there is news of Roger and the others. Speed, for I shall need your help."

In a few moments, John Fortescue entered. His face was grave.

"I fear things have gone seriously amiss, Rex Damory," he said. "We got as far as the New Forest, and there, because my face is too well known, I sheltered with a woodcutter, while Sir Hugh rode on to Dalton Manor. One of the men came back three hours later with the word that I was to go back to Damory and that you would give me a guide to the coast. I do not think that I was followed."

"Here is Roger, my young lord." Rance opened the door.

"Come in, Rance. You will forgive me, my lord. I must know what has happened." Rex spoke quietly, though his hand shook.

"I share your anxiety, Rex. What of Sir Hugh, Roger?"

"They have slain him." Roger, old tired warrior that he was, broke down and sobbed. Rex stood half dazed with the tidings.

When he spoke at last his voice seemed not his own. "Tell me the tale."

"Aye, there is much for you to hear, my lord. We left the messenger at the woodcutter's in the New Forest and rode on to Sir Harry Dalton's place. There two new men joined us, and we started for Lord Medanham's manor house, the country one where they told us he was biding. I did not trust the newcomers, but we were at a loss, and they acted as guides. They led us into ambush. Just in the densest part of the forest, one of them gave a call, and we were surrounded on all sides. I cut the traitor down, but the other reached the enemy. My lord closed his visor: 'Slip away if you can, Roger,' he said in a low tone. 'Get word to the messenger to go back to Rex. I am doomed. Yonder rides my arch enemy.' I followed his glance and recognized Sir Nicholas Leslie. Even at that moment he spoke.

"'Yield, Hugh Damory,' he called, riding forward. 'Yield, or by bright Saint George, not one man of yours will I spare.'

"Sir Hugh hesitated. I knew that he longed to fight it out. But he thought of us.

"'Pledge your word that my men shall go free, Nicholas Leslie, and I will yield,' he said.

"'By my knightly honor, they shall.' Sir Nicholas raised his sword hilt to his lips. 'By the Sacred Sign, I swear it.'

"'I am your prisoner then.' Sir Hugh gave up his sword, and Sir Nicholas bade them seize and bind him. As he stood there helpless, Sir Nicholas spoke to him in triumph.

14

"'My day has dawned, Hugh Damory. You have been taken in arms against our liege lord, King Edward. As Warden of the New Forest, I condemn you to die. Make ready, for the dooms-man awaits you at Southampton. To horse, my men.'

"My lord listened calmly. 'This is unlawful, Nicholas Leslie. The Warden of the New Forest has no right to condemn a state prisoner. I appeal to the judgment of my peers,' he said.

"'A rebel cannot appeal!' Sir Nicholas struck him roughly. 'On, men.' He turned to me. 'Get back to Rex Damory and bid him look to himself now that he knows what the vengeance of Nicholas Leslie means.'"

"And you know nothing more, Roger?" The agony in Rex's voice brought Lord Fortescue to his side.

"I could not follow. There was no chance. My lord, my own dear lord." The great tears rolled down the man's rugged face.

For a moment Rex hid his own. Then with a resolute effort, he choked back his grief.

"We must act now," he said wearily. "There is no time to lose. My lord, will you try for Wales or France?"

"For France methinks, lad. When this affair has died down, I shall make another attempt in London. You had best come with me."

"Not yet. It would not be safe. You may have been followed, and Damory will surely be watched. Roger shall go with you and, when all is quiet, Rance and I will follow later."

"I do not like to leave you here, boy."

"We could not make the coast together, I know. Roger, you must guide. Go over the Roman Road to Weymouth. Charter a fishing smack if necessary. Saddle fresh horses and make haste."

The two squires started on their way. Sir John spoke to Rex.

"You are worthy of your line, boy. God bring you comfort."

"I thank you, my lord."

"Seek me out when you reach France. I will befriend you as

long as I have a shelter myself."

"The horses are ready," Rance announced, and Rex went down to speed his parting guest. Once the horsemen were out of sight, the boy turned to Rance.

"Do you think there is any hope?"

"Scarcely any with Nicholas Leslie. I have seen his vengeance before. What now? Can they not spare you a moment for your grief?"

It was a sobbing boy who flung himself at Rex's feet. "Sir Nicholas Leslie is in Blandford," he cried. "He has come to seize Damory and Damory's men. Red Rose rebels, he calls us, and vows to hang us all."

"What shall we do?" Rance said.

"So this is how he keeps his plighted word," Rex said indignantly. He pulled the boy to his feet. "No tears, but gather the men for us, Simon. We must hold out for terms at any rate."

The boy ran off. Rance turned to Rex.

"You cannot save us, my young lord," he protested. "You will only ruin yourself."

"I share with you all right willingly, Rance. But there is another reason. We have to gain time. Yonder rides the messenger of the Red Rose, the friend of our Prince, and if Nicholas Leslie is not stayed at Damory, John Fortescue is lost."

"Right willingly since that is the case." The squire's face lighted with its old fire. "For England and the Red Rose until death, my young lord."

II

The Siege of Damory

I T WAS a moated fortress which greeted Nicholas Leslie as he rode up the parkway some hours later. He had thought to take the place by surprise, and his face clouded as he realized that this was impossible. But even with the preparations for a defence, he looked for no special difficulty in capturing the manor. He blew his bugle, and Rex came out on the battlement.

"What do you want?" the boy called clearly. "Why have you come hither?"

"I demand admittance in the name of England's King. Admit me and my guards instantly. The King's Grace demands the surrender of the men of Damory to his will. This rebel brood must pay the penalty of rebellion."

"Neither Damory nor Damory's men do we yield in the absence of Damory's lord, Sir Nicholas Leslie. You claim for vengeance law-abiding folk against whom there is no proof of warfare. My father went forth with small tendance on a special errand. He did not resist your demand for surrender and you promised immunity to all his men."

"All is fair in war, my kinsman. It was a good ruse to obtain possession of one who was foe to my liege lord."

"Then are you knight forsworn, false to your oath on the holy Cross and smirched in your plighted honor."

The angry flush rose in Nicholas Leslie's cheeks. He spoke grimly. "You peril yourself, Rex Damory. The score between us is mounting fast. England is a White Rose realm, and your one hope is surrender. By giving up your men, you may win life for yourself in spite of this attempt at resistance. Otherwise you will share the fate of Damory's hinds."

"Right willingly will I company with them, Sir Nicholas. Moreover, you tricked my father. Have I any reason to believe you will be honorable with me? If your tidings are true," Rex's voice shook a little, "the right and the decision is mine own. Unless I treat with the King himself, I hold Damory and Damory's men for England and the Red Rose. Take them if you can."

"The die is cast then. Your manor is confiscate, and you are a rebel. Moreover, I have my own debt to pay and I shall pay it."

"If you can," Rex defied him.

Sir Nicholas turned to his men. "Sound the onslaught, trumpeter. Down with the Red Rose! Fight for the Rose of York!"

The bugle sounded, and the charge came. But after three hours of unceasing conflict, Sir Nicholas was obliged to own himself defeated. Old Damory had been built by Norman hands, and the words and white earnest face of the boy defender inspired his followers. Sir Nicholas was obliged to encamp at nightfall and wait for reinforcements.

Rex had no time for indulgence of his grief. Every hand was set to work strengthening the fortifications, and once these were finished and a strong guard set, the boy with Rance hastened to Sir Hugh's apartments and gathered his papers together.

"A hiding place was constructed some years ago in old Sir

Hugo's tomb, my lord."

Rex followed the squire to the chapel. Rance went to the rear of the tomb and with a lever lifted a stone. A recess lay revealed, and there the two concealed the papers and such valuables as were of small bulk, the gold and jewels, the grant of the manor and other documents. Rance slid the stone in place, fitting it back with care and not leaving it till he had removed all traces of their work.

"You pledge your word to keep this place a secret, Rance?" Rex asked. "Not even if they threaten me, must this be revealed. Documents, gold and jewels, true, are of little worth, but men's lives lie in my father's letters."

"I pledge my word, my lord," the old man answered. "Would that I could compass an escape for you! If we win out of this, I shall not forget, nor will the others, that you have perilled life for us."

"I could do naught else, Rance, and right gladly do I share the peril with you. There is little chance for either of us, methinks. O Rance, pray that I shame not my father, that I keep tryst with him."

"Small doubt of that. You are his second self, my lord." Rance's hand clasped the boy's warmly. A bugle sounded on the air and the two sped to the battlements. Another attack was launched, and the fray lasted long into the night.

The days passed on slowly to the besieged, who rallied loyally about their young lord. Each morning brought relief to Rex, for each day of delay meant safety for John Fortescue. Roger would not be able to win in to Damory, beleaguered fast as it was, though both Rance and Rex feared that he might make the attempt. The fourth day dawned gloomily, for reinforcements came to the besieging host. King Edward arrived with more than five hundred men-at-arms to take the place.

Rex stood on the battlement watching the arrival and the

bustle in the camp of the enemy, when Rance came to him with a grave face.

"I do not trust John Darsten, my young lord," he said abruptly.

"Why not, Rance?"

"I think he is communicating with the foe. I missed him at dawn, and it was a full three hours before he appeared with a tale of having been attacked at the bastion. He has not the heart of a chicken and would never withstand the attack of one man single-handed, let alone the dozen of which he tells."

"But you have no proof of this, Rance. I have never liked him myself, and he is not one of our own folk, as you well know."

"I have no real proof, my lord."

"Then all we can do is to keep watch, Rance. There are no others?"

"He whispered with Rab o' the Dene."

"Another newcomer to my father's household. Give them the guard on the towers, and see that they do not go near the bastion again. We cannot dismiss them, for if your suspicions were unfounded, they would meet with certain death beyond our gates."

"Small loss, methinks," Rance growled. "I do not fear that they will betray Damory, but I fear for you, my lord. If you were safe with the Earl, nothing else would matter."

Rex laid his hand in the warworn one of the squire. "And what would my feelings be, Rance, if I were in safety and you all in peril here? Right glad am I that I may share and share alike in all our dangers. This new move of the foe is serious for us, is it not? It would seem to seal our fate? We can no longer hope to send the foe packing with a sally."

"The nights are dark now, my lord, and we may be able to draw off to the hills. Once in Charlton copse, they would not be able to follow us. That is my hope."

"It seems a forlorn one, Rance. Still we will try it. We will fire old Damory to detain them. But we had best hold out another two days, lest Roger and Sir John be delayed somewhere."

The onslaught that followed an hour later was the severest they had encountered. But again the foe drew off. Damory's walls were strong. But since at last they might be borne back by sheer weight of numbers, Rance and Rex laid their plans. Brushwood was heaped about the towers and combustibles placed within the keep.

"They will put it out, of course," Rance said. "But they will think the papers are destroyed. Damory will not burn easily."

The plan was almost complete when the catastrophe happened. Rex was busy in the house, gathering together such things as might be carried, when just after sunset, John Darsten appeared, face white, dark eyes smouldering with excitement.

"There is a fight at the bastion, Lord Rex," he cried. "Rance is sore wounded."

"Rance!" Rex ran down the stairs, his heart still with terror for a moment. Without Rance what could he do? He forgot the squire's warning nor heeded in his anxiety the steps that followed him. All was quiet, as he stepped out on the bastion, the low embrasure on the left.

"Rance," the boy called, and would have turned, but in a moment two men were upon him. Rab o' the Dene held his throat in a choking grip, while John bound him securely and knotted a rope about his waist. He was swung over the battlement.

"Ready," a cautious voice said below, and all unseen of the tower sentry, two men seized the boy from his captors and bore him swiftly away. John and Rab climbed down in safety. Rex realized as they raised him that he was being carried into the enemy's camp.

He was laid down at last in a tent at the end farthest from the manor. The stifling gag Rab had placed in his mouth was re-

21

moved; his ankle released. He rose to his feet and looked about him. It was a fairly luxurious place, and a knight's chain lay on the table. The low voices of his guards reached him.

"We shall have Damory tomorrow. Truly, Sir Nicholas is a shrewd one to place traitors within those walls months agone. The boy never suspected."

"Silence there, varlets." The stern voice of Nicholas Leslie sounded outside. "You have placed the prisoner within?"

"Aye, Sir Nicholas."

Rex leaned against the tent pole as his foe entered.

They surveyed each other in silence at first. Nicholas spoke at last.

"So now, my lord of Damory, how about no surrender?" he taunted him. "We shall have another tale now, I fancy. Do you still hold your manor, boastful one? Have you no greeting for me?"

"I have no desire to greet you nor to see you, Sir Nicholas Leslie," Rex answered hotly. "I will remind you that although you have Rex Damory, you have not Damory Court."

"We shall see. I have my friends still within the walls. Like your father, you underrate Nicholas Leslie. No one but Hugh Damory would take strangers into his household on a piteous tale, and no one but Hugh Damory's son would be gulled by the tale of a wounded squire."

Rance was safe then and unwounded, Rex thought with relief. And John and Rab, with no one knew how many more, had been paid spies from the first. The trick sent the angry color to his cheeks.

"So as usual since you cannot gain your end by fair means, you use the foul ones which are more familiar to you, Sir Nicholas," he challenged.

"Have a care, my young kinsman. You are a prisoner, remember. Try me not too far."

"I fear you not, Sir Nicholas. You are a perjured knight, false to your oath and to your honor. Do you expect me to respect one who by a lie tricks my father to an unnecessary surrender and captures me by consorting with cowardly spies?"

Furiously Nicholas lashed him in the face with his chain. "That for your insolence, Rex Damory. You know naught of warfare and less of what it means to be a prisoner. But you will learn. You will pay dearly for these insults. Your life is forfeit as traitor to the crown, and I hold the upper hand."

Rex had not flinched for the blow. His hands clenched in spite of his bonds, but he spoke steadily.

"He threatens safely who threatens a prisoner, Sir Nicholas. You had best make the most of your vantage, for there may come a day when Rex Damory will make you answer for this."

"You crow loudly, my young cockerel, but we shall soon see you on your knees. You have your father's craven soul. He too pled for life."

"You lie there." Rex had lost all control of himself now. "You false-hearted craven, how dare you even name him? You struck a woman down long since; you stole from her home a little maid, you in your spite and vengeance sowed Damory with spies. Faith, but your King must be proud of such as you!"

Nicholas shook him into silence, "You shall pay, Rex Damory," he hissed through his clenched teeth. "Forrest and FitzAllen, come hither!"

Two ruffians entered. They were the same who had borne Rex there and now, under their lord's direction, they tied him fast to the posts of the tent. A spearbutt across his shoulders left him as helpless as a trussed chicken, and with a rope's end, they struck him fiercely, till Nicholas bade them cease. Rex made no outcry, and as a call without summoned his persecutors, with a mocking laugh from Nicholas, he was left alone.

The night seemed endless. At first Rex was too angry to feel either the discomfort of his position or fully to realize his peril, and he raged at Nicholas Leslie, as he strove in vain to loosen his bonds. Bruised and weary, he desisted at last and, when the force of his passion died, the memory of his father's parting words came to him. "Death, if needs be for King, for Cause and honor; silence for private wrongs." Well, he was facing death now and a private wrong. He had not kept silence. His head drooped.

"O Father, I have failed you," he said half aloud. "God help me, what shall I do?"

Rex Damory was brave; he came of a noble line, but the prospect was dark indeed, and it was small wonder that in the stillness and silence of the night, his courage failed him. Little did he realize that, as he stood that weary vigil, he was fighting a sharper battle than any he had fought at Damory Court. The humiliation of his capture, the cowardly meanness of his foe, brought the hot temper again and again to boiling point. There were little chances of revenge. Rex winced again. It might even be that he could discredit him slightly with the King. It was only in the dawning that he managed to push his desires into the background.

The sunbeams stole in at the half-opened door of the tent, and Rex realized that perhaps this was the last sunrise that he would ever see. Could he go out to meet his Master with hate in his heart? Unutterably, he longed for shriving and for aid. Would they refuse him all help and counsel? It was no easy task which lay before him, to face an angry King and perhaps to die. Stiff, weary, cramped with his bonds, he waited, praying with all his heart for help and strength. It came. He thought of others, of possibilities for warning Rance and his men. His mind went back to the little maid, the sister, of whom he had just learned. In the hard days which had been his lot, his leisure hours had been occupied with thoughts of her and plans of finding her. He whispered a prayer for her as he waited for the guards.

They came at last. He was released and led through the camp. The soft breeze fanned his white cheeks, as he walked quietly in the midst of the soldiery to the greensward where, in full sight of Damory, stood the King. He was a right royal figure in his gleaming armor, his head bare save for the narrow circlet of his rank. About him stood lords and nobles and, close at hand, a black-visored executioner leaned on his axe near a small block. Rex started as he saw the headsman then, recovering himself, walked on with head held high towards the King.

The guards parted, and he faced the monarch. "Is this the lord of Damory?" Edward asked. "Why this is a lad!"

"A lad in years it is true, but he is nevertheless the Red Rose rebel who has dared to defy Your Grace," Nicholas Leslie answered. "My hope is that his spirit may be a trifle tamed by a night's reflection."

Rex bit his lip, but made no reply. The King spoke sternly.

"What does this high-handed rebellion mean, young sir? How have you dared to defy your liege lord in this fashion?"

Rex bowed respectfully. "Your Grace is no liege lord of mine," he said quietly. "Red Rose am I nor do I deny it. But to Your Grace, I have taken no allegiance."

"You are a rash lad to say this to my face, but let it pass. Your men refuse to yield. Bid them do so."

"Nay, my lord."

"You prefer to die on yonder block?"

"Unless Your Grace will promise them safety and so redeem the broken word of Sir Nicholas Leslie."

"What do you mean by that? These men are fighting against me."

"They fight for their lives, my lord. At the bidding of my father a dozen men-at-arms followed him when he went on a special errand into the New Forest. His surrender to Sir Nicho-

25

las Leslie was made the condition of their freedom and, hardly had they returned, when news came that he was demanding not only these twelve men but all the rest for punishment. We held out against it."

The King frowned. "You told me naught of this, Sir Nicholas? But the fact remains: in peaceful England, Damory has fought against the King, and though I prefer not to war on a willful lad, these men may not go scatheless. They promise to yield at your bidding, Rex Damory."

"May I speak with them, my lord?"

"If they can hear you."

Rex stepped forward. "Rance, Rance!" he called. "Can you hear me?"

"Aye, my lord," Rance shouted back. "Do you bid us yield?"

"Never." Rex threw back his head. "They promise you no safety. Fight on with courage for my father's sake. Beware of newcomers. Fire the manor and fight to the last. Long live the Rose of Lancaster!"

Sheer astonishment at his daring had held the bystanders dumb. Now the great lords sprang forward. Swords and daggers gleamed about the boy, but the King's own weapon struck them up.

"Peace, my lords. The insult is mine, not yours."

The hubbub died at his words, and the courtiers stood back, while Rex faced the King.

"How dare you defy me like this, Rex Damory? Do you think this is child's play?"

"Nay, my lord. Did you not give me a choice? I have chosen."

"A boy's heroics! Is not your life of more importance than those of a set of hinds?"

"Such was not my father's teaching, nor if rumor speaks true, Your Grace's either."

"Well spoken, rash boy." The King hesitated. He looked

26

disturbed for, brave himself, he could well appreciate bravery in others. He noted the boy's steady eyes and undaunted bearing. Nicholas pushed forward.

"Rex Damory has cost us much in time and men," he ventured. "He has insulted the majesty of England."

"If the boy is so dangerous a foe, what will the man be?" Rex heard another say and, raising his eyes, he looked into the pale face and caught the cool calculating glance of Richard, Duke of Gloucester. "Brave he is, I acknowledge, Brother, but he has cost us much already, and it would seem to me unwise to set so staunch a rebel at liberty."

"I have no mind to set him free," the King answered.

"A Red Rose rebel's safest prison is the grave," the Duke answered. "Remember his father."

The King's face darkened, but his keen eyes were turned still on Damory where he had caught sight of a puff of smoke. He turned.

"Troth, but they have obeyed him! Secure the lad, Nicholas Leslie. Sound the onslaught at once, Richard."

With eager haste, Nicholas dragged Rex to a tree and bound him there with his own hands, taking time to see that he was so placed that he could see nothing. There he left him as the struggle began.

"Saint George for merry England! Strike for the Rose of York! Gloucester to the rescue!" The battle cries filled the air while above all rang Rance's shout, "Damory, Damory! Strike for our young lord's sake!"

The shouts roused Rex again. Furiously he strove to loosen his bonds, but they held fast, and at last he desisted, growing more and more weary from his cramped position. The sunlight suddenly faded, and Rex's misery was completed by a downpour of drenching rain. The lurid glow of the flames died down, and the shouts and clangor of battle ceased. Damory was taken.

With straining ears, Rex tried to find out what was happening. *Were they murdering the survivors?* he thought wearily. Then Rance, weaponless and wounded, stood beside him, striving in vain to loosen his bonds.

"Never mind me, Rance, but get you gone," Rex pleaded. "What of the others?"

"Langhorn and Jessop fell beside me, my lord. The others drew off under cover of the smoke and, we hope, are safe. The fire did little damage, and the chapel and Sir Hugo's tower are untouched. What have they done to you, my lord? Oh, for a knife! A murrain on the hand which tied these!"

"You cannot help me, Rance. You will only be taken yourself and will not be able to aid me. Hide in the woodland yonder, till all is quiet, and then get to the coast. Prithee, make haste! Do you not see that you are of more use to me free?"

Reluctantly enough, the squire obeyed. Rex watched him gain the woodland. He was barely in time, for two men-at-arms came forward and with swift strokes of their knives severed Rex's bonds. They brought him to the royal tent where he faced a grim King.

"Your manor is taken, Rex Damory," the King told him. "Now, I want an answer to some questions. Just what did this rebellion mean? How did you induce your men to take up arms?"

"Their lives were in peril, my lord. Would you blame them overmuch for choosing the risk of a battle rather than the certainty of a rope?"

"They be bold for a set of hinds. Such a choice might have been their master's, and I doubt not that your influence went that way, young sir. Moreover, they have made their escape and are in hiding. Where are they?"

"Do you really expect me to tell you? Had my father had fair trial, that might have come out," said Rex quietly. "It is not my business to say. But before my father started on his errand, he told me that any rebellion would be folly."

"We have reason to suppose that other Red Rose lords are involved in this and that Henry of Richmond will be in England; what do you know of this?"

"I have nothing to tell Your Grace."

"You are a bold and obstinate lad and, but for your youth, might well pay the penalty," the King said. "I am not minded to act hastily." He turned and beckoned his young captain of the guard. "Morton, take my lord of Damory and ride for London. Take a sufficient guard with you, and lodge him in the tower to await my pleasure."

Morton bowed and Rex followed him. He was given a hasty meal, and then they started: a strange journey to the boy who, bound to his horse, rode not at his own speed but at that of others. Save for a few hours of sleep at Salisbury, they pressed on and reached London in the sunset of a spring day. There they took boat on the Thames and rowed beneath the Traitor's gate to the grim Tower of London. Rex was lodged not in the prison itself, but in a prison chamber, a fairly large apartment on the third floor of the tower opposite the State apartments and overlooking the royal enclosure. A garden of winding paths lay below with spring flowers bursting into bloom, and as the weary boy threw himself on his couch, he caught the sound of laughter and girls' voices below.

III

The Maidens of the Court

For the wrong so foully done,
Damory's lord must aye atone,
Till maiden's hand bring harmony
And joy and peace to Damory.
And Damory's lord in bitter woe
Conquer Damory's fiercest foe.

THE WORDS sung in a girl's clear voice brought Rex to his feet. The hot July sun had been pouring all day into his prison, and the boy had been sitting rather dejectedly at the table, having pushed aside the manuscript with which he had been ill-treated. His prison chamber was comfortable and the window unbarred; vellum and colors with a manuscript had been provided by a gaoler whose sympathy was aroused by his prisoner's plight. Nevertheless, it was a prison and the weeks had dragged unutterably to a lad used to the freedom of the Dorset Downs.

Till maiden's hand bring harmony,
And joy and peace to Damory.

The fresh voice sang again, and Rex went to the window. Below lay the enclosed garden where he often watched the Princess Elizabeth and her maidens. They were there now, walking in little groups or straying in couples about the paths. Which of them knew of the punishment of Damory?

His unspoken question was soon answered. Two girls came down the path and paused beneath his window.

"Joyce, you have no right to sing that," one of them expostulated. "You know what Sir Nicholas says."

The singer laughed. "You taught it to me yourself, Ruth Leslie, and as for Sir Nicholas, you ought to know by this time that Joyce Deventry does as she chooses without reference to him."

Ruth Leslie, a maiden who had knowledge of *Damory's woe*! Rex felt his heart beating fast, and he peered eagerly from his post of observation at the two girls. Joyce Deventry with rebellious sunny hair clustering about her face, which now was alight with mischief, though he had seen it oft dreaming and dark with thought as he had watched often before. Ruth Leslie was a stranger to him. Tall and slender with something of a likeness to Joyce, her coloring was more vivid. Her hair flamed like an aureole about her oval face which was less pleasing than that of her companion's, for the dark level brows were knitted in a frown, and her brown eyes clouded with anger.

"You sang it yourself, Ruth," Joyce said, teasing her.

"When I was but a babe. Twit me not with that again, I warn you. I am no Red Rose rebel and I scorn their songs."

"It is not a Red Rose song. Nurse Gillian says that it dates back to Norman days and that she learned it from Elsie Leslie herself."

"Who disgraced us all by wedding a Red Rose rebel," Ruth insisted. "I believe you are just the same, Joyce."

31

"I have not wedded a Red Rose man, if that is what you mean."

"You are Red Rose at heart."

"The Red Rose is not in the field, and one can hardly be aught but White now," Joyce retorted shrewdly. "If you mean that I like Sir Nicholas Leslie no better than of old, you are right. He is nothing but a scheming time-server and a cruel-hearted man, and I care not who knows that opinion of mine."

"He is a Leslie, and I will hear no word against him. Moreover, you had best have a care to yourself, Joyce Deventry. Such words as these are dangerous."

"I know that Sir Nicholas has no love for a woman's tongue, but the words are true enough. He *is* a hard and cruel-hearted man. Look at the way he murdered Sir Hugh Damory and, not content with that, holds the poor young lord a prisoner here. The King would have set him free long since, but Sir Nicholas eggs on the Duke with the idea that the lad has important information, and the Duke's influence is paramount with the King."

"Sir Hugh Damory was a traitor, and Rex Damory is another. They deserve their fate. You have gone too far this time, Joyce. We have never been friends, but the parting of the ways has come now. Since we have come here to the court, you have been unbearable. You have supplanted me with the Princess, and you ever plot against Sir Nicholas. Now it would seem that you also are a foe to his Grace of Gloucester! Do you really mean this?"

Rex saw the teasing light go out of Joyce's eyes. Her face was grave now, and she weighed her words before she answered. But the reply was firm and decided.

"I serve our Princess, Ruth. My allegiance is to her."

"That is no answer. Are you a foe to Sir Nicholas or not?"

"Did he ask you to find out?"

"If he did, it was his right. We have been pensioners on his bounty since our babyhood. He has brought us hither and

32

would naturally look for some assurance that we are loyal to him. You ever flout and scorn him. What have you to say?"

"If Sir Nicholas wants to find out my opinions, he can ask me himself, Ruth. I give no answer to you. As for gratitude, Nurse Gillian and my good old grandsire claim mine. Nicholas Leslie does nothing without thought of reward, and, if we have been pensioners on his bounty, it was because he expected a return. As for you, I am willing to be companion and even friend, but I shall not plot against the Princess nor anyone else."

"You are clean daft on the subject of plots, Joyce. I have had enough of this. You never cease to blacken me with the Princess."

"You are talking arrant nonsense, Ruth. This is our old jealousy. I have never said aught against you to the Princess who loves us both. It is ill fortune, or Sir Nicholas who counts for the same, that has placed us side by side here. As for plots, you know full well what I mean, and you cannot deny, unless you willfully blind yourself, that there is one afoot."

"Look to yourself, Joyce Deventry." Ruth clenched her hands. "You insult a Leslie, and a Leslie does not forget."

"Do you mean a blood feud? Your talk is fit for troubadours, Ruth."

"Look to yourself. You are a Red Rose rebel at heart." With a toss of her head, Ruth flounced away. Joyce stood looking after her, till a movement from Rex brought her eyes to his window. She smiled at him.

"Good morrow, my lord," she said. "I am sorry for you."

"I thank you for your kindness, Mistress Joyce. I heard you singing Damory's song; how came you to know it?"

"Ruth Leslie taught me first when we were little maids and better friends than we are now. But I learned about it from my old nurse Gillian, who was nurse to your mother, my lord."

"Joyce, Joyce," the Princess called, and the maiden obeyed the summons, while a heavy hand fell on Rex's shoulder and twisted him from the window. He faced Nicholas Leslie who had entered unobserved.

"So you talk with the maids of honor, Rex Damory. What are you plotting now?"

"Naught, Sir Nicholas."

"Lie not to me. Which maiden was it?"

"I am plotting naught, Sir Nicholas. As for the maiden, she felt sorry for a prisoned lad, who found time hanging heavily, that is all."

"You will come then to the King."

"As you will."

He followed Nicholas down a stairway and into the largest of the State apartments where the King sat at a table with several of his counsellors about him.

"I have brought the prisoner, Your Grace," Nicholas said. "It was high time, methinks, for I caught him in converse with Lady Elizabeth's maid, though which one he refuses to say. No doubt but that he was plotting an escape or worse."

The King frowned. "You seem a true son of a rebel brood, Rex Damory," he commented. "What were you plotting with the maid?"

"Nothing, my lord. I was aweary of my prison and, as I stood at the window, I heard one of the maidens of the Princess say that she was sorry for me. I ventured to thank her. That was all."

"Which maiden was it?"

"That I prefer to keep to myself, Your Grace."

"I am far from content with such an answer, Rex Damory. But we will pass the question by. You have been given ample time to consider and to understand what it means to be a prisoner. I trust you have learned some needed wisdom by the experience. I want a plain answer to this. What induced your father to undertake that last expedition and for whom and to whom did he go?"

"With all due respect, I would repeat that those questions I may not answer, Your Grace."

"I remind you again that you are a prisoner."

"And in Your Grace's hands."

"I can offer you rewards. There lies your freedom, boy. Answer those questions, and you shall have your liberty, your title, and estate."

"That were a poor guerdon for lost honor, my lord."

"Have you forgotten that we have means to make the stubborn speak?"

"God helping me, those things I will not tell. Your Grace must use those means, if such is your will."

"Take him to the dungeons then," the King ordered, turning to Nicholas. "If that does not break his spirit, then we take other measures. Perchance, Rex Damory, this may give you the change that you seem to crave so sorely."

Rex bowed in silence, then with resolute step followed the gaoler summoned by Nicholas and submitted to have the iron chains the man brought fastened on wrists and ankles. The man beckoned him forward, and he stumbled down steep stairways to one of the most noisome dungeons of the Tower. The walls were dank, and the floor was deep in mud and water; toads and rats swarmed everywhere. A faint light gleamed through the grating of a small window high in the wall, and under this, Rex saw a stone couch covered with dirty straw. He sat on this, with a great sinking at his heart. The iron bolts were shot home, and the footsteps of the gaoler died away. The prison grew darker; gradually the hours sped on and the light faded leaving the place wrapped in murky gloom. Rex found himself conjuring weird shapes out of the darkness. Nervous terror shook him repeatedly, and icy hands seemed to hold him in their grasp.

"I shall go mad here," he muttered. But no thought of yielding came to him as he lay on the dank straw shuddering with cold and fear.

35

"Will you answer now, Rex Damory?" Nicholas Leslie's mocking voice spoke at the doorway, and Rex struggled to his feet.

"Never, Sir Nicholas."

The door clanged, and the boy fell back on the couch. He covered his eyes with his outflung arm, and broken words of prayer came to his lips.

"I must not tell. Lord Christ, help me not to tell," he whispered again and again. "Though I die here, keep me true."

It was a bitter hour there in the dark dungeon, but Rex grew calmer at last, and the terror passed as he prayed for courage to meet whatever might befall. Nicholas came early in the morning and found him as determined as ever.

The days dragged on interminably. Twice each day Nicholas came to ply him with questions for an hour, holding out offers of release and ending with a storm of abuse and threats. Rex held out. The rest of the time he was alone, save for the irregular visits of a rough underling who brought him a meager supply of food. But on the third day, his tiny window framed a girl's face, and he looked up into the wistful eyes of Joyce Deventry.

"My lord of Damory," she called.

"You had best not bide here, Mistress Joyce," Rex warned her. "Sir Nicholas Leslie is hunting mares' nests as usual, and he may involve you if you are heard talking to me."

Her eyes brimmed with tears. "I am the cause of your trouble, my lord. I hear the King was angry that you talked with me."

"The fault was not yours, Mistress Joyce. They are asking questions which I may not answer."

"I wish that I could help you."

"It is a help to know that you wish it, Mistress Joyce."

"The King would not hold you fast in prison but for Sir Nicholas and the Duke of Gloucester. They be mad to gain the rest of the 'rebels' or so they say. There be Red Rose lands that they covet still. But the King is generous and likes not to war on lads.

If you had a friend at court, he might win your liberty."

"But I have no friend, Mistress Joyce."

"There is one who might help. I will try. But I dare not stay now. God help you, my lord."

Her words helped him, though Rex could think of no one whom she could enlist in his Cause. But as he sat the next morning thinking of her visit, a new voice spoke through the grating.

"Who is down there?"

Rex glanced up and saw a boy looking down. A gleam of interest came into his weary face.

"I am Rex Damory," he answered.

"The boy who made the defence of Damory Court?"

"Aye. Are you a prisoner too?"

"I might just as well be. I have just come from the Welsh Border, and they watch me well. Why are you down there?"

"I will not give up my father's papers nor his secrets. Sir Nicholas Leslie would involve other Red Rose lords."

"Is that why he is so angry with you? Tell me about Damory Court."

"I have little to tell. I did not see the last fight. My men fired the manor."

"I liked the way you told them not to surrender. I would that we, Yorkists, were more like that. I have wanted to know you ever since I heard the tale. Will you be my friend, even though I am a White Rose lad?"

"Truly, if you care for so useless a comrade. I am like to die in this dungeon even if the King's patience be not exhausted before then."

"Perhaps not. I may be able to get you out."

"I fear that is beyond your power. Only by betrayal of others can I gain freedom."

"I shall try all the same. Alack-a-day, here they come, after me as usual. Good-bye, Rex."

Later that same afternoon, the gaoler entered. "I bring you good tidings, young sir," he said. "You are to be set free, and you are appointed to the household of the Prince Royal."

"I may not serve the House of York," Rex objected, but the man paid no heed. He wrenched the chains off the boy's hands and feet and led him up through long corridors and passages to a suite of apartments. There a guard took charge of him and opened the door of a large room where Rex found himself face to face with his friend of the morning.

"Your Grace," Rex stammered and the boy smiled.

"I surprised you, did I not?" he said. "Do not look so determined, Rex. I know you will not take allegiance nor betray the Red Rose secrets. I only ask your word of honor not to attempt an escape nor to plot with my foes."

"Surely your royal father is not content with that, my Prince?"

"He said your word was your bond. He promised me weeks agone that I could have as companion in my household a lad of my own choice. I have insisted upon having you."

"Yet to serve the House of York—" Rex objected.

"Can you serve the Red Rose better in a dungeon? On my royal word, I will ask no service of you that you are not willing to give. I have few friends and I am lonely here. There is so much strangeness here at court and I need someone whom I can trust. It is as companion and comrade that I want you, Rex Damory. My royal father is so busy; my sweet mother, I seldom see. My sister and I live in this wing together, alone save for our attendants. A weary life it is. Surely you will not refuse me your friendship?"

He held out his hands, and pleading voice and wistful eyes won Rex's heart. The Prince was a tall fair-haired lad, strongly built, who looked older than his years with all the promise of the strength and beauty of the Plantegenets. The blue eyes met Rex's frankly, and the Red Rose lad felt his hesitation at an end.

He laid his hand in Edward's outstretched one. For a few moments they stood looking earnestly at one another.

"True and faithful will I be to Your Grace," Rex promised. "Rescue or no rescue, I will hold myself true prisoner, and I will have no dealings with the Red Rose."

"And true and faithful will I be to you," Edward answered, and thus the compact was sealed.

The Prince led the way to his own bedchamber, and there Rex found that due preparations had been made for his comfort. The master of the wardrobe was waiting with suitable apparel, and Rex was ordered to attire himself in court dress and to be in readiness to attend the Prince when he went to the court that night.

There was high revelry in the great hall as Rex and Prince Edward entered it together. Flaming torches cast a bright glow over rich hangings, and strains of gay music floated from the musicians' gallery. It was an informal gathering, for Edward IV disliked ceremony, and, except in the case of a foreign embassage, his court was left free save for the few who were in attendance upon his person. Animated groups stood chatting in nooks and corners: ladies resplendent in silks and jewels, knights in richest armor, and older nobles in furred cloaks and coronets. The King was seated in a massively carved chair on the dais at the further end of the room with his jester at his feet and he himself the center of a gay throng to whom he talked with careless ease. Nevertheless his keen glance swept the room repeatedly, and he missed nothing. Prince Edward went straight to him and bent his knee before him.

"I greet you, my Father," he said gravely.

The King raised him, and a softer expression came into his face as he took his son in his arms. "How fare you, lad?" he asked.

"Right well, Royal Father. I have brought Rex Damory to you.

He agrees to our terms."

The King's gaze rested upon Rex. "Have I your promise, boy? You will take part in no Red Rose plots?"

"I will hold myself true prisoner, Your Grace, and will take no part with the Red Rose or any other. I pledge my word of honor," Rex answered.

"Way there for our Lady Queen!" The clear voice of the seneschal was heard, and at his announcement all conversation ceased, and every eye turned to the doorway where, attended by her maidens, Elizabeth, Queen of England, entered the great hall. The King advanced to meet her and kissed her hand with courtly grace, for with all his faults, Edward was lover still. His fair wife had well-nigh cost him his kingdom. A chance fall from his horse had necessitated aid at the nearest house which proved to be that of the widow of a Red Rose knight, the Lady Elizabeth Woodville. On his marriage to her, Warwick the King-maker had rebelled and Edward, caught between two armies, had only saved himself and regained his capital by daring generalship.

Rex looked at the Queen curiously. Like others of the Lancastrians he had resented her change of side, ascribing it to her vanity and the glamor of a crown, but now as he saw her fair face and lovelit eyes, he found his dislike melting away. Her young son sprang to her side, and her countenance was radiant with joy as she took her place beside her husband. She sat there, the picture of love and happiness, yet suddenly Rex shivered, for he caught the malignant hate in two crafty, cold eyes and saw the face of Richard, Duke of Gloucester. It was only for a moment that he stood there watching the Queen as the cat watches the mouse before its spring, then the look passed and he came forward, apparently the most devoted of servants.

Prince Edward beckoned to Rex. "My lady mother would speak with you," he said, and Rex found himself under the spell of Elizabeth's glorious eyes.

"So you are Edward's new friend. I welcome you, my lord of Damory," she said. "I know that you will serve him well and loyally."

"I fear Your Grace congratulates yourself too soon," sneered Nicholas Leslie. "Rex Damory comes of a rebel brood and is not the loyal slave that he seems, my lady."

With flushing cheeks, Rex turned on him, but his resentment was not quicker than that of the lovely Queen.

"Peace, Sir Nicholas," she commanded haughtily. "I asked not for your opinion. Yon lad is no traitor; his face speaks truth. Heed not his meddlesome words, my lord of Damory."

"I will strive to merit your trust," Rex said, as he bent his knee to kiss her outstretched hand.

The King laughed. "Troth, Elizabeth, but your power has won the allegiance that threats of death could not do for me," he said.

Rex withdrew with flushing face, but in his heart he knew that the King was right, and that he was in truth a loyal adherent to the White Rose Queen. He stood aside, watching the gay scene with eager interest which was all the greater after the long days of imprisonment, and his spirits rose at the thought of this partial freedom. Suddenly someone paused beside him and looking around, he saw the Duke of Gloucester. The evil hate had died out of his face, and never had he looked more winning. There was an air of comradeship about him as he held out his hand to Rex.

"Let me congratulate you on your freedom," he said. "I ever told my brother that it was a shame to let you die in a prison. Methought that there was some better fate in store for you, and I see that I was right."

Rex stared at him in blank astonishment. The last time he had heard that voice, it had been urging his death. He recovered himself with an effort.

41

"I thank you for your good wishes, my lord," he said, as the Duke seated himself on a low divan and motioned the boy to do the same.

"I have come to give you a friendly warning, lad." Richard smiled winningly. "You will be in no easy position here, and I want to assure you of my help. I will give you whatever I can. But remember this, none hate the Red Rose so much as those who have forsaken her Cause. Ever fair and false was a Woodville."

"Fair indeed to me thus far, Your Grace," Rex answered boldly. "For their falsehood, I must even judge for myself, though I thank Your Grace for your interest and your advice."

"You are a lad after my own heart. I see that you are loyal to the core. You and I must be friends in this evil court where few dare to trust each other. Remember that I stand ready to aid you at any time. Here is my hand upon it."

He rose as he spoke, leaving Rex with a lighter heart at this most unexpected offer of friendship; then as the boy stood watching the Duke pass down the hall, his shoulders were seized in a rough grasp and he was swung round to face Nicholas Leslie. His pale eyes were smouldering with baffled anger, and in spite of his rich garb, he was more unprepossessing than ever.

"And so you have outwitted me again, Rex Damory!"

Rex shrugged his shoulders. "In good sooth, Sir Nicholas, you had altogether escaped my memory. I have not troubled myself as to whether I have witted you or not, for my mind has been full of other matters."

"You had better guard that tongue of yours, my young kinsman. I can do you more harm than you guess now," Nicholas threatened.

"Should I speak you fair or foul, it seems to me that it would matter but little, Sir Nicholas. Your cousinly regard for me is so great, your good offices on my behalf so well known, that a few words could make no difference."

"By what lies have you won this new preferment?" Nicholas sneered.

Rex felt his anger rising. "Ask that question of Prince Edward. My dungeon did not offer many opportunities for speech of any kind. But false as you are yourself, you know a Damory speaks true."

"Again I warn you to beware, Rex Damory. For yourself, mark this, that with all your talk of truth and honor, within two weeks we shall find you as steeped in intrigue as all the rest. Nothing will matter but your own advancement."

"Do you speak from your own experience?" Rex challenged.

With a cry of fury, Nicholas drew his dagger, and Rex would have had the worst of the encounter but for Prince Edward who threw himself between.

"What means this, Sir Nicholas Leslie?" he asked, as several members of the court came up. "How comes it, that you are brawling in the King's presence?"

"Rex Damory insulted me, Your Grace," Nicholas insisted.

"Not so." The Prince spoke clearly. "On the contrary, not only did you insult Rex Damory but also the whole court. You accuse us all of falsehood and intrigue." He laid his hand on Rex's arm and turned away, leaving Nicholas discomfited, for dark looks were being cast upon him and the fiery young Earl of Walsingham was fingering his sword. Nicholas stammered an apology.

"Have a care, Rex," the young Prince whispered as he left. "Mingle with the others, for I trust him not."

Obediently, Rex turned to join with the throng. He stood in the midst half shyly for a moment, then a girl beckoned to him and he crossed over to the side of Joyce.

"I believe I have you to thank for my liberty," he said. "How did you compass it, Mistress Joyce?"

"It was easy. I had heard Prince Edward speak of you and I told him where to find you, my lord."

"How did he know anything about me?"

"Why, do you not know that you are a famous personage? The King himself was pleased to tell your story and your gallant defence of your manor. He did it in the open court."

"That is more to the credit of Damory's men than to me, methinks. All I did was to fall into a cowardly trap. I wish that I were sure that they were all in safety. I think that lack of news is one of the hardest things to bear in imprisonment."

"None of them were taken, my lord. Two men were found dead on the battlement."

"Langhorne and Jessop, I expect," said Rex. "Rance told me that they had fallen when he made his effort to rescue me. He was weaponless and could not cut my bonds. I forced him to leave me at last."

"I think you need not trouble about them. By this time they should be in safety. It is the Red Rose lords who are in peril, but there is no direct evidence of a plot. Right glad am I that you are free, my lord. I blamed myself for a part of your trouble, for Sir Nicholas used my careless words as a pretext to accuse you of tampering with the maids of honor."

"The bottom of the affair was the evidence and Sir Nicholas Leslie's hate of me, Mistress Joyce. But I overheard one thing that day which made me think that perchance you are in my own case with Sir Nicholas. Does he war on others besides Damory?"

Joyce looked around apprehensively and put her finger to her lips. "It is not well to talk of him here, my lord," she said in a low tone. "You do not know the dangers of the court as yet. Your next-door neighbor may be a spy, and unseen ears lurk behind drapery and divan. Some day we will talk more, for we shall see much of each other. The Princess is devoted to her brother, and we live in the same tower. There is little formality and much intercourse, and there are happenings that are passing strange, but these you will find out for yourself. One warning I will give you. Beware of Duke Richard. He is no friend to any of us."

"He has proffered me his friendship just now, Mistress Joyce."

Her face grew white. "Then take care, my lord. As open foe he is far less dangerous than as sworn friend. Everything centers about Duke Richard, and his influence with the King is paramount."

"There is intrigue then, and a plot afoot?" Rex whispered.

"There is more than one, alack, and whether one wills or no, those who serve the royal households are bound to encounter peril," she said wistfully. "But you are brave, my lord, and you will not fear. But here comes my lord of Gloucester. He seldom allows two people to converse uninterrupted."

Richard came up and smiled winningly at them both. "Will you not join the revels with me, Mistress Joyce?" he asked. "I regret to deprive my lord of Damory of his companion, but the fairest lady in the hall must pay the penalty."

"Beware lest your treason be overheard, my lord," Joyce retorted. "Dare you call any the fairest when the White Rose of England graces the hall?"

The Duke's face clouded. Where Elizabeth Woodville was concerned, he was seldom able wholly to disguise his feeling. He recovered himself in a moment.

"Your beauty and loyalty go hand in hand, Mistress Joyce. But the music starts. Let us dance." He led her forward to the center of the hall, and more than one looked in wonder at the great Duke thus singling out a little maid of honor. Joyce read his motives, and though she flushed in embarrassment, as she felt all eyes upon her, she went through the stately measures of the dance with dainty grace. Even the Duke smiled upon her in approval for its duration. At its close, he led her to a seat and placed himself beside her.

"What do you think of the young lord of Damory, Mistress Joyce?" he asked.

"I scarcely know him well enough to venture an opinion as yet," she countered.

"But you talked with him during his imprisonment."

"Only twice, Your Grace. I pitied him as I should any lad of his years deprived of liberty, and I told him so."

"I fear you thought me hard this morning," Duke Richard said. "Your tender-heartedness did not tell you that you were striving to change the King's word. We all must obey our King."

"I am loyal to him as you know well, my lord."

"I believe you are, though like many maids you are impulsive, Mistress Joyce. You do not trust me."

"Have I said so to Your Grace?"

"Not in words, but faces and actions can be read. I know you do not. What do you fear?"

"Nothing that I could put into words, my lord Duke."

"The day will come when you will find how much you have. misjudged me. You are less trustful than my lord of Damory."

"Your Grace is taken with him?"

"I admit that I am. He is a brave lad and a loyal friend. I marvel not at Edward's attraction to him, though I fear his high position will bring him many foes, poor boy."

"Why should the position of attendant bring him foes, my lord?"

"You must know little of court jealousy if you ask that question. It would seem that you do not even know your own influence. You are not a nonentity, Mistress Joyce. An attendant of the Princess Royal is a maiden of importance and may sway the court. For Rex Damory, the position is even greater, for he dwells at the side of the heir of England. But one friend he shall have in Richard of Gloucester. I see that my royal brother beckons me, and I must leave you now." He bent and kissed her hand and crossed to the throne while Joyce sat looking after him with little lines of perplexity on her brow.

"Good night and pleasant dreams to you, Edward," the Duke said as his nephew passed him with Rex in attendance. "I envy you your friend and shall beg the loan of him from time to time."

"Good night to you, my uncle," Edward responded in some bewilderment. "I know that Rex will serve you gladly if need arise."

The two went on and once they had reached the children's tower Edward turned to his companion. "What power have you been employing, Rex, to have won over my uncle of Gloucester?" he asked.

"He was kindness' self to me this night, Your Grace. He sought me out and asked of me friendship."

Edward knitted his brows. "What has changed him so suddenly, I wonder? Why did he oppose me so bitterly this morning and then prove himself your ardent friend tonight? He used every argument at his disposal to keep my father from granting me the boon of your release. He turned on poor Joyce when she acknowledged that she had spoken to you and scolded her till the maid wept. But I held to my point and won. Well, my royal uncle has puzzled wiser heads than mine."

"I am sorry indeed that Mistress Joyce should have fallen into disgrace on my behalf. Who is she, my lord?"

"A maiden who attends my sister. She is a puzzle to most of us, for she was foisted on Elizabeth directly through my uncle of Gloucester's influence. We liked it not till we came to know Joyce and found how true and loyal she is. For some strange reason, my uncle seems to dislike her thoroughly. She is wise with a wisdom beyond her years. You will have to find out about her for yourself, Rex. As far as that goes, Ruth Leslie is another mystery and a less pleasing one. There be many strange things about the court and some of the strangest lurk about the children's tower. But we must rest."

Rex asked no more questions, but he lay sleepless for many hours that night. The change which the day had wrought was a great one. Last night he had slept in a noisome dungeon; now he shared a prince's chamber. He thought over all the happenings of the past hours and fell asleep at dawn thinking of the strange maid named Joyce.

IV

The Plot

THE DAYS that followed were pleasant indeed to Rex. The companionship of another lad was a new experience to a boy who had been alone all his life, and, in spite of his sorrow for his father, there were hours in which Rex's laugh rang out as merrily as Edward's own. After the long days of idleness, the sharing of the Prince's studies was a joy, and Father Gemort, the gray-haired tutor, rejoiced at the progress they made. The quiet of the children's tower was seldom disturbed. The King's health was daily growing more precarious; the Queen was in close attendance upon him, and the daily visit of authority was generally made by Duke Richard. To Rex he was ever affable and friendly, frequently taking him away on rides and walks where his flattering interest and charming manner did much towards winning the lad's love.

That Rex did not wholly give himself up to this friendship was due to the evident distrust that the other children had for the Duke. Edward frankly disliked him; Princess Elizabeth avoided

49

him; and Joyce was worried and uneasy in his presence. For Joyce, Rex's liking was rapidly ripening into friendship, and for the Princess he had a growing loyalty and love. Only one person stood aloof from him. Ruth Leslie disdained the "Red Rose rebel," and her tongue lashed Rex in shrewish fashion. At last there came a day when Rex, returning from a ride with the Duke, found Edward in an undeniable temper.

"Our peace is at an end, Rex," he greeted him petulantly. "My uncle has persuaded my father that my little brother, Richard, is old enough to share our sports, our rooms and our studies. He is but a babe, barely ten, and it is ridiculous."

Rex laughed at the Prince's woe-begone face. "Is it as bad as that, Your Grace?" he questioned.

"Aye, it is. What can I do with the baby wanting to share in everything? I am no child's nurse nor are you. Besides there is something behind it all. My uncle of Gloucester never does anything without some dark reason."

He sprang up as the door opened and the Queen entered. Her face was very pale, and her eyes were reddened with recent tears.

"I have come to speak to you about Richard," she said, as the boy put eager arms about her. "I had hoped that he would be left to my care for some time to come, but my lord of Gloucester has persuaded the King, your father, otherwise. Guard him well, Edward. He is such a little lad."

The Prince's face was crimson as he kissed her again. "Fear not, I will take care of him, mother of mine," he promised. "Rex will help me. I was grumbling about it sorely a few minutes ago, but I am sorry and will do so no more."

"Edward, Edward, Brother!" A little fair-haired lad of ten ran in. "I am to be with you always, always. You will teach me everything, will you not? I want to be just like you."

"Surely, little Brother." Edward drew him close, and their

mother kissed them both.

"I trust you, Edward," she said earnestly. "Now lend me Rex Damory, my son. I would have his escort back to mine own apartments."

Rex sprang forward eagerly and flushed with pleasure as she rested her hand upon his shoulder. Outside the door, she drew her cloak about her, muffling her face, taking a back path through the gardens to the royal tower. As they entered, she drew Rex into a sheltered buttress.

"My lord of Damory, I fear there is a plot afoot," she whispered. "In three days' time, the King plans to make a progress through the City of London, and for the first time, Edward is to go with him. You will also be in attendance. Look well to the Prince and watch closely all who approach him. Especially have a care to my lord of Gloucester. My heart misgives me for the safety of my son."

"I will guard him with my life, Your Grace."

"I know that and I trust you. Now one other question. How came you to make so bitter a foe of Sir Nicholas Leslie?"

"He has sworn a blood feud on the Damorys for my father's sake, Your Grace. It was fancied wrong in the first place, but through it, my sweet mother died. My twin sister was stolen away. I know but little of my father's fate and I, myself, would have perished in a dungeon but for Prince Edward."

"He is leaving no stone unturned to harm you here. Thus far, he has made no progress. Be watchful and guard yourself lest he take you unaware, heed all that men say and do, and, as you value my safety and Prince Edward's, tell no one of my visit to the children's tower or of my warnings to you today. Promise me."

"I promise," Rex answered, and she smiled and turned away. He stood watching her as she went up the stairway. Then a hand was laid on his shoulder, and he turned to face the Duke of Gloucester.

"Who is yon lady who parted from you just now?" asked Richard.

Rex laughed. "A secret of mine own, my lord."

"You evade me, Rex. I asked a question. That was some minion of the Queen's, and it behooves me to know what plot my fair sister-in-law is concocting now. Who was the lady, and what did she say?"

"That I may not tell you, my lord. This much I can say. Our conversation was of private import, and Your Grace is not concerned in it."

"Then you prove false to me, Rex?"

"It is not falsehood, my lord, but I have pledged my word."

The Duke's face grew dark. "And so you choose your paltry word before my friendship and perchance, my life?" He gripped Rex fiercely. "I will give you one more chance. Refuse, and you and Richard go on separate paths. Friend or foe, lad?"

"Foe then, Your Grace," Rex answered steadily.

"So be it," was the icy reply, and the boy shivered at the hate in the steel-blue eyes that met his. This fury that died in stillness was terrifying. The Duke passed on and Rex stood still, biting his lips and heavy at heart.

"What are you doing here, Rex Damory?" The questioner was Lord Woodville, brother-in-law to the Queen. "You look troubled, boy."

"I am troubled, my lord," Rex answered frankly, as he threw back his head and met the nobleman's searching gaze, eye to eye.

Lord Woodville sighed. "You are very like your father, lad. But for that fair hair of yours, I could almost think it was my old comrade, Hugh Damory, and that we were boys again in Lord Erskine's train."

"You knew him there, my lord?"

"We were close friends. Like him I incurred the hate of Nicholas Leslie, for I testified against him after the affair of the rose garden."

"And he hounded my father to his death."

"Overstepping his authority and risking his position at court by that same deed. The King is just, and his indignation rose hot when he heard of Sir Hugh's execution. Nicholas Leslie would have been dismissed and mayhap imprisoned but for Duke Richard."

"You loved my father; will you then for his sake counsel me?"

"Right willingly, lad."

"The whole story I may not tell, for I pledged my word to silence. I promised to keep a secret and one, who called himself my friend, bade me tell him or forfeit his friendship."

"What did you do?"

"I kept my word as I believe my father would have done. But still the broken friendship weighs upon me."

"You were right in your choice. The one who put you to such a test was no true friend to you, Rex Damory."

The boy sighed in relief. Lord Woodville put a kindly hand upon his shoulder. "Keep up your courage, lad, and go on as you have begun. Fear not Richard of Gloucester while I live."

"You heard then, my lord?"

"Nay, the riddle was not hard to guess. I have known Richard of Gloucester and his ways too long. Now go, lad. Remember I stand your friend."

Slowly Rex made his way back to the Prince. But he was not needed. With little Richard, Edward was with his sister in the garden, and Rex walked between the limes to the river bank. The boats were sailing up and down the river, small sailboats, river craft and large poled barges. It was a busy scene. He stood watching for a few moments till his eyes fell on Joyce Deventry as she sat under a tree looking out into the distance with wistful eyes. As he approached her, she sprang up in alarm.

"Is aught amiss with the Princess?" she cried.

"Nay, Mistress Joyce. She is safe enough with Prince Edward

and her little brother. Morton is on guard and Mistress Ruth in attendance. We are not needed. You must not always think me the bearer of bad tidings."

She flushed as she re-seated herself and made room for him beside her. "I have some reason for my fears," she said. "If I knew just what to anticipate I should be less afraid. You spoke of little Prince Richard. Methought he was with the Queen."

"His Grace of Gloucester has persuaded the King that he should share his brother's quarters now."

Joyce went white. "Then he is ready to strike," she said under her breath. "O Rex Damory, guard your Prince well."

"Do you know of any definite danger which is threatening him? All seem alarmed. The Queen herself is troubled, and yet I cannot make out what it all means."

"You have not been at court long enough, and Duke Richard treats you as a friend."

"No longer, Mistress Joyce. Less than an hour ago he declared himself my foe."

"Then he could not have his way with you. I told the Princess that he would not. You are in like case with me."

"Does he war on maids?"

"On any man, woman, or child who stands in his way, my lord of Damory."

"It is Rex just now. May we not be comrades, Joyce?"

She held out her hand. "We will stand together, Rex."

He clasped it warmly. "What is this danger, Joyce?"

She put her finger on her lips. "Do you not realize that but two lives lie between Duke Richard and England's throne?" she whispered.

"Prince Edward and his brother? What of the King?"

"He will not live long, so say the wise leeches. The danger lurks about the royal children, Rex."

"But there are four of them."

"True. But with the Red Rose always in the background, England is not like to call a Princess to her throne. If aught befell his nephews, Duke Richard would be King."

"Would he murder them, think you?"

"The Duke of Clarence died long years agone within these walls." She pointed at the round tower behind them. "It is common rumor that Duke Richard was the cause. He fomented the trouble between the brothers. The pardon that he bore came an hour too late."

"But surely that brought him into disgrace."

"There were excellent reasons. His horse fell lame. He was mobbed in the city. He broke away and rode at full speed and long way round but George, Duke of Clarence, heir to England's throne, died."

"I see. I will keep good watch and ward."

Joyce shivered. "I am afraid of Duke Richard, Rex. Those he hates do not live long."

"We must keep brave hearts, Joyce. I will stand by you to the very end."

She smiled. "It is easier now you are here and know, Rex. I have felt so alone. There seemed no one to help me."

"Does not Ruth Leslie help you?"

"No one ever knows what Ruth will do. First and foremost, she is a Leslie, and because Sir Nicholas is one, he can do no wrong in her eyes. Ruth loves the Princess, but even in that case, she would stand by her kinsfolk because she is a Leslie."

"I wonder if she is."

"What do you mean by that?"

"Part of Sir Nicholas Leslie's vengeance on Damory was to carry off my twin sister, Ruth. We were both about six then. I am trying to find her."

"Do you think that she is Ruth Leslie?"

"I have no proof or any likelihood of getting one at present.

Sir Nicholas will see to that. Why do you laugh?"

"It ought not to be a laughing matter. But in truth, Rex, you would have no monotony in life if this should prove true. Ruth hates a Red Rose rebel."

"She has made that very clear already. But she knows *Damory's woe*, at least I heard you singing it one day below my prison, and you told her that she had taught it to you."

"She did when we were small maids together. She lived with an aunt and I with my old grandsire and Nurse Gillian. Leslie Manor is a rambling old place about five miles from Leslie Grange where Ruth lived. We were often together. Our household was a strange mixture of kinsfolk who drifted home. Sir Nicholas fell heir to the manor soon after your mother's marriage. He has never been there much himself, but his family feeling is strong, and he has always been generous with his own people. There Ruth taught me *Damory's woe*, and I sang it in his hearing one day. He turned on me, white with rage. He is angry, Rex, and he vows that Damory has been his punishment. That *Damory's lord in bitter woe, would conquer Damory's fiercest foe*, has always been his fear. He thought your father might escape him, and now he has turned on you. Being a teasing little child, I plagued him with the song, and so he insists that I am a Red Rose rebel at heart."

"Who is Nurse Gillian, Joyce? And how did the Leslies happen to come to Devonshire? Surely the name is a Scotch one."

"The Leslies are Scotch. Ronald Leslie, your great-great-grandsire, was captured and held prisoner with James the Fifth of Scotland in the reign of Henry IV. Like his master, he married an English maid, and because she was an only child and he a younger son, he settled men-at-arms, among them a certain Ralph Murray. His granddaughter is Nurse Gillian who came as nurse to your mother and has stayed ever since. She is the most loving and loyal person imaginable with her grandsire's Scotch speech, and she is the only person of whom Sir Nicholas stands in awe. He obeys Nurse Gillian and has a vast respect for her plain speaking."

"I should like to know her. Is your grandsire still living, Joyce?"

"He died two years ago in the great fever. Ruth's aunt died too. Then the Torsmen began to give trouble, and Ruth and I were sent to court. This intrigue against the Queen began a year ago, and Sir Nicholas seemed to have an idea that we, maids of honor, would help him in his plans. I did not, and though Ruth is not hostile to Sir Nicholas, she loves the Princess Cecily sent to Castle York with her nurse, but the King insisted that Princess Elizabeth should stay at court. But hark! The Prince is calling you."

Together they made their way back to the royal children. Elizabeth was pouting. "I would that I were a lad and could go on a progress too," she said.

"Some day you shall go on one with me, sister mine," Edward promised, and her face cleared.

"Then I will wait," she promised, and ran off hand in hand with Joyce.

"We are to go on a royal progress through the City of London tomorrow, Rex," the Prince said. "My uncle has given orders that you are to ride beside me, and we are to be surrounded by my own Welch guard. The King will ride ahead with his own men; my uncle with his will bring up the rear. I have never seen the city. This will be a wondrous treat."

It was early the next afternoon that they set forth. At the head rode the King with his bodyguard all wearing his personal badge of the rising sun. Next came the young Prince with his cortege of Welshmen, Rex riding slightly behind him. Last followed Duke Richard with his formidable band of tried warriors, clad in green and silver with the silver hog of Gloucester on their arms.

Behind came the City Guilds, the floats, and the yeomanry. The procession passed at a footpace amid a cheering throng. All went well along the broad path of the river, but in the narrower streets it was harder to keep together. Suddenly they turned into the Cheap, and, as they turned, by some mysterious management, the Welshmen disappeared, and the men surrounding them wore Duke Richard's silver sign. Rex looked around vaguely alarmed, and rode closer to the Prince. Then he bent forward listening. Mingled with loyal shouts was one more familiar to his ears, the slogan which had nerved the men of Damory in their last stand. It was only a murmur at first, then without any warning it filled the air in a mighty shout, "For England and the Red Rose! Down with the House of York!"

For a moment consternation reigned. A mob of ill armed but numerous folk surged forward, and the King's guard engaged. Then with a shout of "Gloucester to the rescue!" the Duke swept by, joined by those about the Prince. Edward spurred onward with Rex striving to regain his place, but Duke Richard turned. With his own hand he pushed the Prince and Rex roughly aside and slashed their horses with his riding whip. The frightened beasts turned in the wrong direction, and the two lads found themselves in the midst of a whirling throng who jostled, bruised, and bewildered them as they shouted with all their might, "Death to the House of York!"

Quick as thought, Rex tore the white badge from Edward's cap and hid the golden lions on his tunic by flinging his own cloak about the Prince.

"Up, Giles man," he shouted. "Spur your horse; there is work for merry knaves today. Saint George, Saint George, for England!" He pulled his companion's rein and turned into a side street.

"We are lost, Rex," Edward cried. "It is a plot with our lives for forfeit."

"Not yet," Rex answered cheerily. "We will make trial for sweet liberty first."

"How now, my masters? Whither aways so fast?" Strong hands checked their horses, and they found themselves surrounded by yeomanry. "Who are you?" demanded their captors. "What are you doing?"

"Pages, so please you, fair sirs," Rex answered. "I am Rex, son of Sir Hugh Damory, and my companion is Giles, son of Lord Llathgorn of Wales."

"I know him," said a bystander. "A right valiant knight is my old lord and one of the true Cause. I saw him not an hour agone."

"You speak sooth, good sir." Rex bowed low. "His son follows in his steps. A staunch adherent of the old Cause is Giles of Llathgorn. But, by my halidom, the moments are passing. Prithee, speed us on our way. My lord brooks no dallying."

"Let them pass. Good fortune go with you, lads."

"Gramercy, noble Sire." The two rode on quickly. "Faith, Rex, but you were taken aback when yon man called out he knew my father." Edward laughed. "What Cause is it that I espouse so valiantly?"

"I would that I knew." Rex smiled ruefully. "That there was such a name I never guessed when I made it up, and as for the Cause—well, I follow it with you, noble Giles, though I know not what it is. I only hope my old lord will keep out of our way. If we could only find out which side was which. These may have been White Rose men, but I dared not take the chance. I thought my own name might give us a clue, for the Red Rose knew my father, and the White are aware that I am your attendant."

"What does it all mean, Rex? Do you think the Red Rose is in force?"

"It is a senseless proceeding if they are. They have no chance of success. The worst of it is that the crowds are so thick on the river. Do you know any other way back to the Tower?"

"Not from here. But yonder is a City Gate. If we could win through that, we could shelter at some hunting lodge in Epping Forest."

"Who comes?" a guard challenged them sternly.

"Friends," Rex answered. "I pray you detain us not. Our errand is of importance, and the crowd has delayed us already."

"None pass without the countersign, young sir."

"I have no time to tarry over countersigns. I am Rex Damory. Let me through at once or take the consequences."

"The Yorkist King could not pass here tonight."

"It is not night nor am I the Yorkist King," Rex retorted. "Let me pass, fellow, or evil will befall you when those in authority learn of your delays."

The man slowly unbarred the gate. "Tell me more of your purpose and perchance I will let you through."

"It is not for your ears," Rex replied haughtily.

"When the gates swing open, dash through," Rex whispered to the Prince. He watched the man slowly unbarring the portal. The guard turned on him again.

"Shall I risk my neck for two rascal pages? Tell me whither you go or I will lodge you both in the city prison."

Rex surveyed him with cool insolence. "Were you aught but a yeoman knave, I should chastise you. You are an inquisitive varlet!"

"Tell me your errand," the man thundered.

"Curiosity is ever a dangerous thing," Rex drawled. "It once killed a cat, so the good wives say, and a cat has nine lives while you have but one."

The gate fell open with a crash as the man lunged at Rex. With a swift blow, Rex knocked the halberd aside and rode after the Prince through the unguarded gate.

"Thank the Lord that you are safe!" Edward cried. "I expected every moment that he would strike you down. Why did you anger him so?"

"I knew if I made him angry enough, he would leave the gate unguarded, which is just what he did. Moreover, we are safe from pursuit, for he will not dare to report such a breach of his own orders. Troth, but his face was a study when I repeated the adage."

"Are you never afraid, Rex?"

"Very often, Your Grace. In this case, I could have done nothing but die with you, had you not followed so swiftly. If we talk of debts, I am still in yours, for did you not rescue me from prison and from torture? Is that a light over yonder?"

"It is, and this is the royal hunting lodge. I have been here before. Ride up to the door, Rex. We are safe at last."

In a few moments they were in the small house. The old verderer made them welcome, apologizing for the lack of tendance by saying his sons were away on a hunt. He gave them the best that the house afforded but said he had heard naught of any disturbance in the city. Over an ample meal, the two boys discussed the puzzle.

"Who could have started such a riot?" Edward asked. "It came all of a sudden and at the most awkward place."

"I do not think that it was really Red Rose at all," Rex answered. "Henry of Richmond is in exile, and there was nothing to be gained in a city riot. That cry was a blind to hide something else."

Edward sat thinking hard. "I believe my uncle of Gloucester is back of this," he said at last. "He hates me, Rex, and I am in his way. My own Welshmen melted away like mist in the wind, and it was his hand that pushed us both back into the mob. He lashed our horses, too. Of course he will explain it. He always does."

"I do not see how he could compass a thing like this, my

Prince. Your lady mother warned me there was a plot in the wind, but I do not see how Duke Richard could manage a Red Rose rising."

"If my uncle of Gloucester wants a Red Rose rising, he will have it, though no one will ever find out how he managed it." Edward laughed. "Come and sleep, Rex, for we must be early afoot tomorrow. We have got to get back somehow."

The "somehow" caused a sharp argument at the morning meal when the lads broke their fast.

"You had better stay here, my Prince. I will ride to the city and strive to reach the King," Rex insisted.

"I would rather go with you, Rex. I do not like being left alone here. Such an idea is folly."

"With all due respect to you, the other is worse. You know how difficult it was to get out. It would be almost impossible for two of us to get in again unobserved, and, while we may suspect many things, we do not know just how far-reaching this rebellion may prove to be."

"Well, I like it not, but if you will promise to come back to me as soon as you have delivered the message, I will bide here. Promise me to come back with the guard."

"I promise," Rex answered as the old man entered. "I am going to the King, verderer, and I must leave the Prince in your care. Have you any weapons?"

"Only bows and arrows, my lord."

"Then take my dagger." Rex handed him his jewelled weapon with the arms of Damory carved upon the hilt. "You will defend him?"

"With my life and at all costs."

Feeling less anxious for the promise, Rex sallied forth, riding rapidly towards the city but slowing his pace as he came in sight of the gates. Just as he reached them, they were flung wide and a troop of men rode out. The boy's heart throbbed with relief as he caught sight of the White Rose badge, and he was undismayed even by the fact that the leader was Nicholas Leslie. He reined in his horse, and his kinsman spurred up to him. Nicholas laid a heavy hand upon his shoulder.

"Rex Damory, I arrest you in the King's name, on a charge of high treason."

"On whose accusation forsooth?" Rex cried indignantly.

"His Grace of Gloucester's. The charge is that of kidnapping the Prince Royal and of inciting a rebellion in the City of London."

Rex's eyes blazed for a moment. Then he spoke, controlling himself with a manifest effort. "I am innocent, and you know it, Sir Nicholas Leslie. But the Prince himself will clear me. He is on this road in the royal hunting house of Epping."

Nicholas seemingly paid little heed to his words. He turned to his men. "Bind the lad fast, and carry him to the King. FitzAllen, Forrest, and Thorsby, follow me."

Rex bit his lip as the men seized him. But he spoke quietly. "I surrender myself, Sir Nicholas, and await the King's pleasure."

Again Nicholas made no rejoinder but followed by the three men he had called set off down the road. The rest of the band bound Rex still more securely and set off for the Tower where their arrival was at once reported to the King. Rex was led to him at once. It was the same audience chamber where he had faced the monarch before, but a far grimmer assemblage awaited him now. The King, white and worn from an anxious vigil, sat at a small table. On his left was Richard of Gloucester, at his right, Lord Woodville. Other attendants stood in the background, and the soldiers held the boy tightly.

"You have played us false, Rex Damory," the King thundered. "Where is the Prince?"

"Safe, my lord, where we took shelter from the mob last night, in the royal hunting house in Epping. Sir Nicholas Leslie has started to bring him back."

"How did you happen to take him there?"

"The rush of Duke Richard's men, when he went to your help, pushed us into the mob, my lord. I threw my cloak over his lions, and we made our way to the city gate as the way to the Tower was blocked. We reached the hunting house and, finding that we were safe, stayed there for the night. This morning because I feared that the riots might be continuing in the city, I left Prince Edward with the verderer and came to tell you the tidings, Lord King. I was arrested as I reached the outskirts of the place."

"A clever tale," sneered Duke Richard. "What of the Red Rose plot, Rex Damory?"

"I know of no plot, Your Grace."

"And do you expect us to believe all this? Does it not seem strange that after these many years during which the King has made repeated progresses that the first time a Red Rose rebel rides with our Prince, a Red Rose rising occurs in the city?"

"It would be stranger still if the Red Rose rebel could compass it, after four months' imprisonment of the closest kind and a few weeks of semi-freedom in a closely guarded tower, Your Grace."

"You are too quick with your replies, Rex Damory," the King interrupted sternly, and Rex bowed at once.

"I beg pardon if I have transgressed, my lord. I will content myself with the statement that I know naught of any Red Rose plot and leave the clearing of my name to the Prince."

"Who is not here as yet," Duke Richard reminded him.

The King's brow darkened. "If harm befall him, Rex Damory, you shall die in such torment that death shall be welcome," he threatened.

"And I shall be content to do so." Rex looked him full in the eyes. "If aught befall Prince Edward, life will not be a valuable boon to crave. Red Rose rebel as you term me, the outlook will be but dreary without my one friend."

"You still insist that you know nothing of this plot?"

"I do, Your Grace. Since my imprisonment, on my word of honor, I have not spoken with a Red Rose man."

"You do not speak of maids," Duke Richard interposed sternly. "What of Joyce Deventry?"

"Mistress Joyce Deventry has never spoken of politics with me, my lord Duke. If she is Red Rose, I know it not."

"She is Red Rose, nevertheless, obstinate child that she is," averred the Duke. "Doubtless, she has acted as the go-between."

"My lord of Gloucester," said Rex steadily, "I have known enough of the Red Rose in past days to be sure that the leaders are not wont to use, in plot or rising, lads and maids. Moreover, the riot of yesterday was no Red Rose plot. The cry was not genuine enough."

The Duke suddenly changed color, and the hate that shone in his eyes for a moment showed that the words had gone home. He recovered himself with an effort.

"We get nowhere thus," he told the King. "Best send the young upstart to cool his heels in a dungeon cell for a time."

The King assented, for Duke Richard's influence was paramount, and illness had robbed him of his wonted keenness. He turned to the guard and consigned Rex to a prison cell.

It was not the noisome dungeon of other days, but dark and gloomy enough. There Rex waited through an endless day. He started at every sound, expecting the door to open and Edward to come to his side. Whether Prince Edward would be able to clear him of complicity in the supposed plot was a question he well knew, but he felt sure that he would make the effort. But as the hours passed on, Rex's anxiety grew. Could aught have befallen the Prince? Was he not to be permitted to see him? It was not until late afternoon that Rex was summoned to the King.

He entered the audience chamber with a light step and a confident air. But no welcome sounded in his ears and, with growing uneasiness, he glanced about him. There stood the King, Duke Richard, and Lord Woodville, but not the Prince. Nicholas Leslie entered by another door.

"My lord of Damory, where did you leave the Prince?" asked the King sternly.

"In the royal hunting lodge in Epping Forest, Your Grace."

"He is not there," said Nicholas Leslie.

"He was there when I left. Ask the verderer; he will acknowledge it."

"I think not. Your plot was complete, Rex Damory."

"I tell you, Sir Nicholas, that I know naught of a plot."

"You know naught of a plot, Rex Damory? Yet the Prince is gone and the verderer lies murdered."

"Murdered!" Rex staggered back, white to the lips. "The verderer is murdered? God help us all! Where is the Prince?"

"Well acted!" Duke Richard turned the lad to face him. "This is useless, Rex. Confess at once or suffer."

"Punish me as you will, I can tell you no more, my lord. I left Prince Edward at the hunting lodge while I sought help from London. The verderer was alive and vowed to protect him. Sir Nicholas Leslie, with three of his own men, sought him and must have found him, for I had left him but a half an hour before."

"Cleverly told," sneered Nicholas Leslie. Duke Richard laughed in biting contempt. Suddenly, Rex turned on them in a gust of indignation.

"I know it all now," he cried. "The plot is yours, Nicholas Leslie, yours and my lord of Gloucester's."

"The boy is mad," said Richard coldly.

"Peace all," ordered the King. "Sir Nicholas, tell your tale."

"I sought the hunting lodge after I had arrested Rex Damory,

Sire. It was empty, but after some search I found the verderer lying dead with this dagger in his heart. It bears the arms of Damory. I recognized it at once."

He held it up, and Rex sprang forward with a startled cry. "It is the dagger that I left with the verderer."

"You see that he acknowledges the crime," Nicholas triumphed.

"I do not," Rex retorted. "The verderer told me that he was without a weapon, and, fearing lest some of the rioters come by or robbers attack the place, I gave him my dagger for the Prince's protection."

"Wrangling will not help you, Rex Damory." The King calmed him again. "You acknowledge this dagger to be your own?"

"I do, Your Grace."

"You swear this tale to be the truth, Sir Nicholas Leslie?"

"On my knightly word, it is the truth." His eyes fell beneath the contemptuous gaze of his young kinsman.

"Why did you delay so long in Epping, Sir Nicholas? You have but just returned, I understand."

"I made a search, my lord. We explored the paths and the woods and questioned the passersby on the highway. There is not a clue."

"I see. What have you to add to this, my lord of Gloucester?"

"I saw Rex Damory draw the Prince's bridle rein when the cry for the Red Rose was first raised. By main force, he dragged him into the mob and then turned into a side street. I should have followed but that my help was needed at your side, Brother."

Pale indeed but quiet now, Rex listened as they swore his life away. The King turned to him.

"What have you to say, Rex Damory?"

"That I am innocent, Your Grace."

"You still refuse to confess? You still will not tell us what has become of Edward?"

67

"Would that I knew!" Rex's voice shook. "I have told you all the truth."

"No more of that." The King now held himself in stern control. "You have lied and foully, Rex Damory. You must take the penalty of your crime. Your guilt is clear. You were last seen with Prince Edward. By your own admission, we know that you were at the hunting lodge, where the verderer has been found murdered with your dagger in his heart. You are proven guilty of treason and that despite your plighted word, also of the unprovoked murder of an old man too feeble to resist your cowardly attack. Your life is justly forfeit, and I doom you accordingly. By right, you should be sent to Newgate Gaol and hanged from the oaks of Tyburn, but because the name you bear is old and honorable, I will spare you that. You will suffer on Tower Hill at the Headsman's hands. I stay the execution only till we gain some clue to Prince Edward and his whereabouts. If none be found in two days' time, we must try sterner measures to make you speak. I offer you your life and mayhap your liberty if you will tell us how to bring Prince Edward home in safety."

"And gladly would I place my head on the block this instant to do that, Your Grace," Rex said. "For the rest, I submit me to your will."

He bowed and followed his guard back to the narrow prison cell where his last days were to be spent. The King looked after him.

"The boy is true Damory," he said. "He bears himself like warrior tried. Can he be speaking true?"

"I should test him on the rack at once," Duke Richard interposed. "A turn or two of that would bring another tale, I fancy."

"Most likely, it would not," the King answered thoughtfully. "The boy has shown no fear of pain or death. There is something, too, in what he said about opportunity. How could he have started this rebellion?"

"My own suspicions rest on the maid, Joyce Deventry," said Duke Richard. "They often conversed together."

"The lad is clever enough to formulate the plans, and the maid could act as go-between," insisted Nicholas Leslie.

"But as we can find no ringleaders, I see no possible proof of this statement," objected the King. "Do you think Joyce Deventry knows anything of Edward's fate, Richard?"

"I doubt if she does, but the boy may tell her if he has the chance. He has talked much with her, and the maid did not deny last night that she shared a secret with Rex Damory. I have it, my brother. Let her visit him in the prison and arrange that their conversation be overheard."

"That is easily managed. The Queen asked me this morning if she or one of the maids might not have speech with Rex Damory. She shall send Joyce."

Unknowing of the plan to trap him, Rex sat in his prison striving to face his doom. It was hard to die, all the harder now since he had had the taste of liberty and freedom and companionship. He shivered at the thought, but it was not the pain which whitened his lips and drove the color from his cheeks. The agony lay in the shame. To all, the memory of Rex Damory would be that of a lad who had committed foul murders, who had betrayed one who trusted him, and who had blackened the noble name that he bore. Then, there was the Prince. Where was Edward? Was his fate as bitter as his own? Rex buried his face in his hands, and slow tears trickled through his fingers. His heart was sore too for the old man who had welcomed them so kindly, struck down by despicable hands.

The grate of the key in the lock and the rasping of the bolts as they were pulled back brought him to his feet as the door opened to admit Joyce Deventry. Her face was as pale as his own, her eyes reddened with many tears, but she strove bravely to smile as she held out her hands to him. He held them close in his own.

"You are good to come to me, Joyce. You do not believe this tale?"

"Do you need to ask? The Queen herself believes you, Rex."

"I thank you both for that." He pulled a rough stool forward. "It is safe for you to come to me here? The Duke was trying to involve you today."

"It is safe enough, for the Queen herself sent me. In any case, I am not afraid. Rex, where can Prince Edward be?"

"If I only knew! I have racked my brains, Joyce. Would that I had not left him for a moment! In my own thoughts, I suspect Sir Nicholas Leslie; yet I cannot think that even he would have been daring enough to harm or kidnap the Prince Royal after the plot had failed. It must be that the robbers of the forest have captured him."

"I do not agree with you there." Joyce spoke resolutely. "Sir Nicholas came back unattended. Who went with him?"

"Forrest, FitzAllen, and Thorsby."

"His own men from Devonshire. I know their reputation of old."

"But what would they do with Prince Edward? They would not murder him?"

"They would hardly dare do that in England, I think. But he is doubtless a prisoner. O Rex, it is hard to be so helpless!"

"I know. That is the hardest part for me. If I knew that he were safe, I could face death more calmly."

"Death, Rex? They will not kill you?"

"I am under sentence. Nay, weep not, Joyce. Pray that I may have strength to meet it."

She choked back a sob. "I will not cry and make it harder, Rex. If I could only help you!"

"You do, Joyce. But my heart misgives me for you too. You are in fresh danger now yourself."

"I am not afraid if only the Prince is found. I will not give way like this. God can take care of you still, and I believe that He will. Perchance this is but *Damory's woe.*"

"And maiden's hand bring harmony
And joy and peace to Damory,"

Rex quoted sadly. "You have brought it, Joyce. Remember that, whatever my befall. Now one thing more. Bid the Queen beware Duke Richard. It was his hand that thrust Prince Edward back and left us to the mercy of the mob."

"Do you think that the whole plot is his?"

"I do, and his henchman is Nicholas Leslie. Duke Richard's following in the city is a great one, and I see now that if he wished to raise the Red Rose cry, nothing would be easier. Prince Edward's Welshmen melted away to the rear at his bidding, and we all know that his bodyguard follows him without question. My fear now is for little Duke Richard and Princess Elizabeth."

"She is in less danger than the little Duke," Joyce answered. "I am afraid that they may have spirited Prince Edward to France. There he would be lost or slain in some chateau dungeon. Fortunately, in this alarm, the King is insisting that the little Duke bide with his mother, and he is well watched at present. I wonder how they have compassed it all."

"And the Queen herself?"

"She is wondrous brave, though we all see the heartache and terror in her face. She loves her children, and her heart breaks over them, Prince Edward missing and Lady Cecily in Castle York."

"Well, warn her concerning Duke Richard, Joyce."

"You had best rule your tongue when my lord of Gloucester is the theme of it, Rex Damory." Nicholas Leslie flung the door wide and stood there scowling at them both.

"What are you doing here, Sir Nicholas?"

"My duty. I have been listening, Rex Damory."

"And what have you gained?"

"Enough to ruin you and the girl, too, if I choose."

"Then you had best choose, Sir Nicholas. You cannot attaint either of us of treason," Joyce suddenly confronted him.

"You cannot deny that you are a Red Rose rebel even as he is, Joyce."

"With you and your notions of honor as a sample of the White, it is a temptation to join the Red," she retorted. "As a matter of fact, I have not."

"And you do not know where Prince Edward is?"

"I do not. Moreover, I am not here to bandy words with you. Come with me, Sir Nicholas; we will go to the King."

"I do not choose; I hold my hand, Joyce."

"Nor do I choose that you should wait for your vengeance. If you do not come, I shall go alone, Sir Eavesdropper."

"You will repent it. He is in no mind to listen to traitors."

"I am glad of that, Sir Nicholas."

"You have spoken treason of Duke Richard."

"Treason consists in speaking against and plotting against the King, Sir Nicholas Leslie. Both Rex Damory and myself believe that the Duke of Gloucester is at the back of this plot and that the knowledge of the Prince's whereabouts lies with you. Neither you nor Duke Richard rules England as yet."

"What is all this coil?" The King entered the room. "Sir Nicholas, have you gained aught from the boy or from the maid?"

"Speak, Sir Nicholas," Joyce ordered him. "He listened at the door, Your Grace, and then came in to accuse us both of treason."

"Rex Damory said that Prince Edward was in France."

"Pardon me, Your Grace, but Rex Damory did not say that. I opined that if the White Rose wanted the heir to England out of the way, he would be taken to France. You know that to be true."

"Why do you say *White Rose* plot?" Rex spoke quietly and respectfully. "It was no Red Rose hand that threw Prince Edward and myself into the mob."

"Look for Forrest, FitzAllen and Thorsby, my lord. Why did they not return with Sir Nicholas Leslie from the hunting house?"

"Who are these men, Sir Nicholas?"

"Rascals of mine, my liege, who have joined my lord of Gloucester's troop. I believe he has sent all three into Devonshire for a few days."

"Summon them back for questioning, Sir Nicholas. Rex Damory, you have twice tried to throw this stigma on my brother. I will hear no more. Beware, lest you involve Joyce Deventry in your treason."

"I will say no more, Your Grace." Rex looked into the King's angry eyes. "God can bring home the Prince in safety and make mine innocence clear. For the rest, if Your Grace believes me guilty of this plot, then send me the doom which I deserve. I do not ask for mercy for myself and I need not for Mistress Joyce Deventry. Her only fault is friendship for a Red Rose rebel, and we of the Red Rose know that England's King does not war on maids."

The King eyed him sternly. "You speak boldly, boy," he said at last. "Joyce Deventry, get you back to the Princess Elizabeth. For you, Rex Damory, time must show, but I counsel you to make ready for death, for your crime is not one which will win forgiveness."

V

The Prince

IN THE meantime, where was the Prince? Nicholas Leslie found him at the hunting lodge as Rex had predicted. "Where is Rex?" was his first demand.

"In London, Your Grace," Nicholas answered.

"I told him to return." Edward spoke petulantly.

"Why have you brought my lord of Gloucester's guard and not mine own?"

"To save time, Your Grace. Prithee, take what escort is possible in pity to the King's anxiety. I, with Thorsby, will delay a few moments here, but Forrest and FitzAllen will see you into safe keeping."

"I like it not, Sir Nicholas, but for my father's sake I will go," Edward said, as he mounted his horse and rode off with the two men. They went on in silence for some time, then the young Prince reined in his steed.

"This is not the road to London," he said, and would have turned. In a moment, FitzAllen had caught his bridle and Forrest bound his arms behind him.

"Traitors both," Edward cried, then glancing at their badges, "So this is my lord Gloucester's doings."

FitzAllen nodded maliciously.

"Villians," muttered the Prince, "and greater villain he who egged you on. Whither are you taking me?"

"To France," Forrest informed him with a grin.

"Where is my lord of Damory?"

"In your own case."

"A prisoner. Not dead then?" Edward's eyes brightened.

"Not yet," was the ominous answer. "He may be suffering."

Edward shuddered. Then he fell silent, striving to brace himself for his own fate. It was a prospect to fill his heart with terror for in France, in the hands of his foes, he knew that nothing but assassination could await him. His heart misgave him, too, for his little brother who must now face added dangers as the heir to the throne. Once the Prince of Wales was dead, only the life of the child lay between Gloucester and his ambition. Yet, in spite of sad thoughts and homesick weariness, Edward faced his trouble royally, bearing himself so well that his captors turned from mockery to respect and their taunts ceased.

During the day they kept to the woods, but at nightfall, they turned into the King's Highway and rode on briskly. It was midnight as they neared the gates of Canterbury, and the bells of the great cathedral rang out on the still air. Edward pulled himself erect at the sound and looked longingly at the little town so still and silent in the moonlight, Dane John's mound in the distance, and the stately abbey, under the graceful spires and ivy-covered cloisters of Canterbury's cathedral. Forrest checked the horses and brought them to a walk, in order to avoid the notice of the watchmen stationed near the gates. They pressed nearer to the cathedral, where the shadows fell, and a sudden hope sprang into Edward's mind. If he could only claim sanctuary!

He threw himself heavily against FitzAllen with closed eyes.

"A murrain upon it, he has fainted, and in a town at that!" the man exclaimed. "There is wine in my saddle-bag. Lift him down and lay him on yonder bank. I will get it."

Forrest obeyed, but no sooner did the man let go than Edward sprang up and, before either of the ruffians could realize his intention, he had dashed at full speed into the cathedral. Through the choir of kneeling monks he ran, crying as he did so, "I claim sanctuary! I claim sanctuary! I appeal to the judgement of God!"

The Archbishop himself came and stood between him and his pursuers. "What has he done?" he asked.

"It is a young lad whom we are taking to France," Forrest answered boldly. "He is mad and may do himself or you a mischief, and his friends would have him in safekeeping."

"He has claimed sanctuary, and so his case must be adjudged," said the Archbishop. He turned to the boy who was kneeling, hands clinging to the altar. "What is your story, lad? What! Is it possible? The Prince of Wales?"

"Aye, the Prince of Wales," Edward returned. "I have been made prisoner."

At the Archbishop's recognition, the two miscreants fled before the astonished monks could stop them. Edward was taken to the little room at the right of the altar where those who took sanctuary were lodged.

"How came Your Grace in this plight?" asked the Archbishop.

"There was a disturbance during the Public Entry, my lord. The King was attacked, and in the melee, I was left behind in the midst of the mob. The quick wit of my personal attendant, Rex Damory, saved me, for he flung his own cloak about me and got me out of the crowd. The way to the Tower was blocked, and we gained the hunting house in Epping Forest and lodged there for the night. Rex left me to seek aid, and while he was gone, I fell into the hands of these cowards. We travelled hard all day but, thanks be to God, the rascals feared to go through the town itself, and I was able to elude them and get into the cathedral."

"You had narrow escape indeed. This attendant of yours, my Prince, is he the son of Sir Hugh Damory of Damory Court?"

"The same. He is true as steel to his father's Cause. A Red Rose rebel they term him, but he is more faithful to me than many a sworn liegeman. Do you know aught of him?"

"I heard of his defence of his manor, and I knew his father well. There is one here who is still more interested in the lad than I am myself. Father Oswald, Prior of the Augustinians, has grieved sorely over Sir Hugh's death and has longed to succor his son. In Lady Elsie's lifetime, he was chaplain of Damory and knew Rex as a little lad."

"I should like to see him, my lord. Rex has been so lonely, and to hear of anyone connected with the old days would rejoice his heart. And yet I know not even if he lives, for he fell into the same cowardly hands that I did myself."

"We will hope for the best. Now, you must rest, my Prince, and I will see Father Oswald. He would be the safest to carry the message to London, for he is ever to be trusted and can keep a silent tongue. Your royal father must be well-nigh distraught."

"He will be, and he is ill too." Edward spoke in troubled tones. "I must start myself with the dawning. I know you will give me an escort. But be sure, Your Grace, that the Father Prior gives the message to none but my father himself. Moreover, bid him say that if I should fall in with my lord of Gloucester's men, I shall take refuge in the nearest church."

"I think I can promise you a strong enough escort for you to have no fear of stragglers," said the Archbishop, smiling. "These caitiffs who bore you off will make good their escape lest your uncle's strong hand fall on them in vengeance."

"Perchance so," was all the comment Edward made and, a few moments later, he was asleep.

IN LONDON the search continued, none more eager in it than His Grace of Gloucester and Nicholas Leslie. Hour after hour, the messengers came into the council, and the King's face grew more weary and haggard as time passed on and the cry was still, "No tidings."

"If the boy would but confess," muttered the King at last.

"I believe he is innocent," Lord Woodville suddenly interposed. "I do not believe that Rex Damory knows where the Prince is any more than we do."

"Who could trust the improbable tale that he tells?" jeered Nicholas Leslie.

"I can," Lord Woodville answered calmly. "Rex Damory showed no want of sense when he defended his manor. Why, if he murdered the verderer, should he leave his dagger and calmly direct Sir Nicholas to all the evidence which would incriminate him?"

"You are strangely credulous, my lord," sneered Duke Richard. "Beware lest we put a new construction on your defence of this traitor."

"I am convinced that he is innocent," Lord Woodville reiterated. "And were we looking for those in conspiracy, I am not the one whom the life of the Prince of Wales affects most nearly."

The Duke crimsoned. "Is this insult directed at me?" he thundered as he drew his sword.

"If the cap fits you, wear it," Lord Woodville retorted.

"Peace, my lords," the King interrupted sternly. "Will you dare to wrangle in my presence? Lord Woodville, leave us, and you, my lord of

Gloucester, keep silence; can you do naught but wrangle in the court?"

Lord Woodville bowed and withdrew; Duke Richard kept haughty silence.

A page came in. "A messenger has just arrived from His Grace of Canterbury, lord King."

"I cannot see him now."

"He says that his message will not brook delay, Sire, nor may he give it to anyone else."

"Bring him hither then, but woe betide him if he disturb me for naught."

Father Oswald entered, and the King greeted him curtly.

"What trouble now with His Grace of Canterbury? Have the stubborn monks defied his authority again?"

"All is well with His Grace, Sire. He sends you greeting—"

"Is this a time for messages of empty compliment?"

"The Prince of Wales is at Canterbury, lord King."

"What?" The King sprang to his feet. "Edward is safe at Canterbury? Thank the Lord! Thank the Lord! An escort instantly!"

Duke Richard had risen from his seat. His face was very pale. "I will see the strongest is sent instantly," he began.

"I have not yet completed my message," Father Oswald interrupted. "The Prince bade me say that he would start for London this morning and should reach here at sunset, unless he fell in with any of my lord of Gloucester's men, when he would seek sanctuary in the nearest church."

"A strange whim! What does it mean, Richard?" asked the King of his brother.

"I cannot understand." The Duke looked puzzled. "But let him have his way. Send your own guard, my brother. Doubtless, Edward will explain himself."

It was late that evening when the Prince rode in. He was tired and travel-worn, and his father looked anxiously at his pale and weary face, as he embraced him again and again.

"Thank the Lord, I have you safe, my son," he said. "The Red Rose has stolen your color, Edward."

"I know naught of the Red Rose, royal Father, but too much of Gloucester's silver hog."

"I greet you, fair nephew," interposed the Duke, coming forward. "This is a glad day for us all."

Edward shrank away, avoiding his embrace. "Greeting to you, my uncle of Gloucester. Why did you wish me in France, if today is so joyful a one for you?"

All eyes turned on the Duke. "What do you mean, Edward?" he asked uneasily.

"You know my meaning full well," said the Prince. "Will you dare to deny that your hand thrust me into the midst of the howling mob where, but for Rex Damory's bravery, I had lost my life? Will you aver you did not plan to send me to France under the care of FitzAllen and Forrest, who declared openly that they had kidnapped me by your own orders? Deny it not, my lord Gloucester, your face proclaims your guilt."

The Duke laughed harshly. "This insult to me would be serious, if it were not absurd. Do you jest now?"

"It does not seem a jest," began the King.

Prince Edward turned to Nicholas Leslie. "Where is Rex Damory?" he asked. "You said he was safe, Sir Nicholas, when, at the royal hunting house, you had inveigled me into your despicable trap."

"You were at the hunting house after all?" asked the King.

"Of course I was. Did not Rex tell you so? Where is he?"

"In the Tower prison, sentenced to death for his treachery to you, my son," said the King.

"Treachery to me!" The angry color flushed into Edward's cheeks. "He thrice saved my life, and, were it not for him, I had been in my grave today. Sir Nicholas, you told me he was safe."

"When have I seen Your Grace?" asked Nicholas. "I came

to the hunting house to find the verderer murdered with Rex Damory's dagger in his heart."

"Then you or the villain, Thorsby, must have murdered him," Edward cried. "I left you talking with him, when I rode away with those two miscreants."

"Your Grace must be dreaming. I have not seen you since the day of the entry. As for Forrest, FitzAllen, and Thorsby, they have deserted, have they not, my lord of Gloucester?"

"So I was told today, Nicholas." The Duke spoke gravely. "In our grief over our young Prince here, I had not heeded my own loss overmuch."

"But you were there yourself, Sir Nicholas," Edward insisted. "You excused yourself from attending me, because you had to talk with the verderer—I supposed about reward."

"Someone has masqueraded," said Nicholas perplexedly. "Methinks this Red Rose plot was more far-reaching than we thought."

"Who could have masqueraded?" queried the Prince.

"I fear it is some plot of my young kinsman," said Nicholas sadly. "I had hoped he was about to mend his ways, but this does not look like it."

"You credit him with unusual power," said the King. "Whether he be mixed up in the plot or not, it would seem a remarkable performance for him in a prison in London to have personated you in the hunting house of Epping."

"Such a thing is possible," urged Nicholas.

"Stop, Sir Nicholas," the young Prince spoke hotly. "Your hatred of Rex Damory, we all know. Those who hate, use all means. Rex Damory left me a full hour before you came to the hunting house. Moreover, I know the men in question and they are my lord of Gloucester's."

The King frowned. The Duke stepped forward, grave and self-possessed.

"It is a base conspiracy against me," he said sorrowfully. "Edward, lad, I doubt not you believe every word that you have said, but you have been strangely misled." He bent his knee before the King, and his melodious voice deepened with emotion. "My lord, my royal Brother, you have heard the accusation against me, and to you and to your justice, I appeal. I have fought beside you; obeyed your least command, and, I ask, have you ever in word or deed found me aught but loyal to you and to your house? If you have the slightest doubt and believe me capable of this traitor's plot, I ask no further trial by peers and equals but pray you to send me to instant death. I waive all appeal to the laws of England, for in life and in death, Richard is ever your liegeman, brother, and servant. My life is in your hands."

There was silence as he ended, and the King's stern eyes grew gentle during his appeal. He bent forward and raised him.

"I believe you from my heart, Richard, my Brother. As soon would I believe myself capable of this despicable deed as you. Rise, I trust you fully."

"I care not now, though all the world should count me traitor." Richard kissed his brother's hand. "You will take my word for Nicholas. I have known him and tried him well. This is a Red Rose plot to sow dissension between us. FitzAllen, Thorsby, and Forrest are rascals. We are well rid of them."

"That must be the explanation," said the King. "Bribed by the Red Rose, they kidnapped my son."

"And the Red Rose rebel had best be made to speak," said Richard. "Rex Damory is traitor, that is clear."

"He is no traitor," Prince Edward spoke earnestly. "On my royal word, he left me at the hunting house, and, but for him, I had died on the day of the entry. It is no Lancastrian plot. I know that he is innocent. You have taken the word of my uncle concerning Nicholas Leslie. Does mine count for naught? I tell you, Rex Damory has won your thanks and not your scorn.

Moreover, he is clear of the murder of the verderer, for *he* was alive when I left the hunting house."

"You are right there, and his story agrees with yours. I can refuse you nothing today, Edward. He can have had naught to do with this. Morton, fetch the boy hither."

In a few moments Rex came in. His face was calm enough, and he walked straight to the King, looking neither left nor right.

"Rex, Rex!" Edward sprang forward, and into Rex's eyes and pale face flashed a transfiguring joy.

"My Prince, my Prince, you are safe! Nothing matters now. I can die in peace."

"The Prince has pleaded for you, and you are free, Rex Damory." The King spoke coldly and Rex stood almost in a daze as the chains were wrenched from his hands. The room seemed whirling about him; he clutched at the Prince, swayed, and knew no more.

"Father, royal Father, is he dead?" Edward cried.

"Nay, he is recovering now. It is only sudden shock. The strain of these days must have been terrible for such a lad, brave as Rex Damory is."

Even as he spoke, Rex had recovered his senses and was struggling to his feet. "I thank you, my lord," he said quietly. "I crave your pardon for this scene. I did not mean to play the coward thus."

"Go to your own apartments and rest you," the King said, more kindly. "Edward, my son, your mother and your sister wait for you."

"I will go to them, royal Father." Edward kissed the King's hand. As he turned to the doorway, the Duke of Gloucester intercepted him.

"You doubt me still, Edward?"

"Have I not reason, my uncle?" His clear gaze met the Duke's, whose eyes fell.

"And you are less generous than the King?"

The boy held out his hand. "If I have wronged you, I am sorry, my uncle," he said, and passed on.

In the meantime, Rex reached the children's tower. A cry of joy greeted him.

"Rex, Rex, you are safe!" Joyce ran towards him with hands outstretched.

"Safe and reinstated, thanks to the Prince," Rex said.

"There is someone waiting for you, Rex." Her eyes shone. "Father Oswald of the Augustinians, who says he knew your mother."

Rex sprang eagerly up the stairs. The grave Prior rose.

"You do not remember me, Rex?" he said. "I should have known you anywhere, lad. You are your father's self again, save for your fair hair."

"And you loved my father?" asked the boy wistfully.

"We were close friends, Rex, and ever since I heard of his death, I have longed to succor his son. I sought the Archbishop to plead your Cause, but then we heard that Prince Edward had done so successfully."

"He has been kindness' self to me," said Rex. "But for the missing of my father, these last weeks have been happy ones indeed. Only sometimes I wonder if I am wrong to serve the House of York."

"I trow not. You are true to your Cause. Yet, lad, think not overmuch of party quarrels, but strive to make peace through your young Prince."

"In truth, Father Oswald, our danger lieth less from the Red than from the White."

"So I judged from what the young Prince said. Your duty is plain enough. You must stand by him in all things. But remember, if aught befall that you have to leave the court, there is a welcome and a refuge for you at Canterbury."

"I thank you indeed for that. Danger there is I know: if Nicholas Leslie can compass it, I shall never reach man's estate."

"Does he hound you too?"

"He never forgets or forgives. It is almost an obsession with him now, and he is determined to block me in my search for Ruth. But I have a clue."

"Beware, lest he involve you with the Red Rose. He may know, like the rest, that there is an effort to revive the Cause in the young Earl of Richmond. Well, farewell, lad, remember I stand your friend at all times." The good Prior rose, and Rex accompanied him down the stairway. Suddenly Father Oswald started.

"Who is yon maid?"

"Joyce Deventry, attendant to Princess Elizabeth."

"Is she your clue? She has a look of your fair mother."

"She is kin to the Leslies, and that might account for the likeness. My clue is Ruth Leslie, another maid of honor."

"I see. Well, good fortune to you, lad, and God keep you." The Prior departed, and Rex would have gone up the stairway but for the sudden interruption of Ruth Leslie, who confronted him, cheeks aflame, eyes flashing.

"By what right do you bandy my name with riff-raff, Rex Damory?"

"The Prior of the Augustinians of Canterbury asked me a question, Mistress Ruth. He can hardly be termed riff-raff."

"What did he want to know? I am aweary of these secrets. You are pleased to be mysterious with Joyce Deventry, and I demand a reason. What is this clue forsooth? You plot and involve maids in your plans, Red Rose rebel that you are."

"I have no objection to telling you." Rex spoke haughtily. "I am seeking for my twin sister, Ruth Damory. Not content with wrecking our home and causing the death of my mother,

Nicholas Leslie, coward that he is, stole her away that night, hid her among the Leslies and probably gave her his own name."

Her words came in a torrent. "You mean I am your clue? You would ally me with a Red Rose rebel? I hate you, Rex Damory, and cry you scorn. Dare not to speak of me or to me. I will never own you as kin. I am a Leslie."

"As was my mother, Mistress Ruth."

"One false to her people, wedding a Red Rose rebel!"

Rex suddenly turned on her. She had angered him at last. His face was flushed and his eyes ablaze with indignation as he caught her wrists. For once Ruth was face to face with a fury equal to her own.

"In faith, Ruth, you pass bearing," Rex thundered. "Do you never rule that shrewish tongue of yours? It is a relief indeed to see that you bear no marks of Damory save a stolen maid's name, and by my troth, I grudge you that! My mother was noted for her gentle courtesy; my father for his nobility of speech and character. You are no rightful clue, you proud girl. You belong with Nicholas Leslie and all his ilk. Damory wants you not."

She wrenched herself free. "You shall pay for this, Rex Damory," she stormed. "Your mother's gentle courtesy and your father's noble speech have small part in you, coward and bully that you are! I hate you and I will ruin you yet."

He took her by the shoulders and gave her an angry shake.

"Enough of that," he commanded. "Henceforth you will rule your shrewish self where I am concerned. Keep your tongue silent in matters of my doings, or I will go to the King himself and tell him how you play the spy and are the tool of Sir Nicholas Leslie."

Ruth gasped. For once she had met her match. She suddenly huddled on the steps in a gust of helpless tears. Rex was too angry to care for her weeping. He turned on his heel and left her with a gesture of contempt.

She sobbed on while he went upstairs and paced the corridor, striving to master himself sufficiently to return to the Prince.

VI

Red Rose Intrigue

"WE MUST rid us of Rex Damory," said Nicholas Leslie.

"Easier said than done," returned Duke Richard. "Edward has more influence than I thought, and he fights like a very wildcat where Rex is concerned."

"Our plans are at a standstill, Your Grace, so long as Rex Damory is attendant to Prince Edward."

"I know." The Duke frowned. "But I see no way to dislodge him unless we can attaint him of treason."

"Then our way should be clear, my lord. We have only to involve him in this Red Rose plot."

"He will not join. He has this ridiculous loyalty to his plighted word, Nicholas."

"Bait the trap with my young lord of Richmond and you will see."

"How can you manage a thing like that?"

"Our spies tell us that an emissary of Henry of Richmond is

in hiding with the Red Rose lords in the neighborhood of London, Your Grace. Circulate the suggestion among the retinue of Lord Medanham and Sir John Dacre that this young springald is in a position to help them, and then give them an opportunity to reach him. Give him his liberty, and keep close watch on him until we trap him."

"It is worth the trial. Send FitzAllen to the Red Rose, Nicholas. He is a shrewd rascal and none too nice as to conscience. Ruth Leslie will aid in watching the lad. She has a hate for Rex Damory which almost equals your own."

"She is a Devon maid, and Devon folk do not forget."

"I cannot understand your own hate, Nicholas." Duke Richard surveyed his henchman thoughtfully. "Why do you take such trouble over this boy? I should have rid myself of him and sent him to the block long ago."

"With all your shrewdness, my lord, you do not understand the hate of a Torsman. We, Leslies, are Dartmoor folk. To kill Rex Damory would not be enough. I want to see him broken at my feet, pleading for the mercy that I will not give."

"If I know aught of humankind, and I know men, you will never gain that desire. Rex Damory will never cringe before you. Did his father?"

"A murrain on him, no! Hugh Damory ever defied me. But I will have my vengeance on his son. Well, I will set FitzAllen to work."

He departed, and the result of his plans soon began to cause uneasiness to Rex.

"I wonder why the guard has been lightened, Your Grace?" he asked Edward. "Why are your Welshmen suddenly withdrawn by my lord of Gloucester's orders?"

Edward looked up from his book. "Have you not been long enough at court to know that there is no accounting for my uncle of Gloucester or his orders either, Rex?"

"I learned that very soon, Your Grace. But this makes me
think that there is something in the wind. For the first time, I
am left to follow my own devices unwatched. Does he want me
to escape? In good sooth, I have nowhere to go."

"Nor would you, if you had." Edward rose and flung his arm
lovingly about his friend. "You are hunting mares' nests and the
wild, wild goose, Rex. It is probable that my uncle knows that he
can trust you and needs the guards elsewhere. There is trouble
on the Scottish border, and troops have started thither every day
this week."

"I like it not. My lord of Gloucester does not do things without a reason," Rex began, then turned as a guardsman stood at
the door.

"There is a man below who asks to have speech with my lord
of Damory," he announced.

"Who can want me?" asked Rex.

"Go on and find out," Edward suggested. "Look not so troubled, Rex. You are finding plots in everything today."

With a laugh to disguise his own uneasiness, Rex left the Tower and descended the stairs to the courtyard to find his visitor
waiting. He was a tall man, muffled to the eyes in a travelling
cloak. He turned at the sound of the boy's step and drew his
disguise down. Rex sprang forward with a rapturous cry.

"Rance! Rance!"

The squire bent down and kissed his hand. "My lord, my own
dear lord," he faltered.

"You are mad to venture here, Rance. Where have you been?"

"In France until a month ago when I came back and joined
Lord Dacre. I have been sent here to ask your aid, my lord."

"I am a prisoner, Rance. Who sent you?"

"The Red Rose. The word came to Lord Dacre today."

"The Red Rose blooms?"

"At Lord Medanham's." Rance dropped his voice. "You will

help us?"

"I cannot, Rance. My word is pledged."

"You have not turned traitor, my young lord?"

"No, but I have given my parole and my oath to Prince Edward to have no dealings with the Red Rose."

"But our Cause may depend on this."

"I cannot help it, Rance. I cannot help it."

"You gave your word to your young Prince. This concerns the Princess."

"My word was given to England's King. I am not asked to give up my Cause or to take allegiance, but I am bound as a prisoner to take no part in plots."

"The Red Rose will not understand."

"You who knew my father so well, Rance, know what he would counsel here."

"Sacrifice all for your word. You are like him, my young lord."

"I must follow his teaching, Rance, come what may."

"My heart misgives me for your safety, Lord Rex. Your own side may take revenge for this."

"I must abide the issue." Rex spoke steadily. "You had better go at once, Rance. A guard may question you."

"I passed within right easily. It is good to see you again. Lad, lad, my heart has been sore for you!"

"And I have grieved sorely for you, Rance."

The squire bent and kissed his hand again, then slipped away, while Rex stood looking after him in anxiety and perplexity. What was he to do now? Must he act? The plot concerned the Princess Elizabeth, and he could not stand by and leave her unwarned. Yet to tell the King might bring ruin on the Cause he loved. He went slowly up the stairs in search of Joyce. That she would keep his secret he knew well. He knocked at the door. Joyce herself came out.

"Is anything amiss, Rex?" she asked.

"I am in trouble, Joyce. A Red Rose plot has come to my knowledge. How and what it is I cannot tell you, but within it is a plan to harm Princess Elizabeth."

"Is there danger for the Prince?"

"I think not. I do not know the plan but only that the plot is against the Princess."

"We must warn her, Rex. She is in the garden now."

The two sped down the stairway and out into the garden. The Princess was nowhere to be seen.

"Where is she?" Joyce gasped. "Ruth should be here, too, and where are the guards?"

A sudden scream rang out and Rex pushed his companion aside and dashed full speed towards the postern gate. He saw two men hastening out, one carrying the Princess, while the other kept guard.

Rex flung himself on the man who carried Elizabeth and almost succeeded in releasing her, but the other man turned back and struck him a vicious blow with the flat of his sword. Rex fell stunned, as the men, paying no attention to Joyce, ran through the gate and entered a waiting boat moored near the wharf.

The King, seeking his wife's apartments, heard Joyce's scream, and, followed by Morton, his personal bodyguard, made his way at once to the garden. He found the girl sobbing over Rex, the gate wide open and the Princess nowhere to be seen.

"Where is your Princess, Joyce?" he asked sternly.

She sprang to her feet, while Morton bent over the boy.

"She is stolen, Your Grace. Rex and I heard her scream and saw the men carrying her off. Rex attacked one, but the other struck him down."

"Which way did they go, Joyce?"

"There was a boat moored near the wharf. They rowed towards the city."

"They cannot have had much start. Morton, summon the

guards. Where is the man who should be at this gate?"

"There was no guard there when we came through, Your Grace," Joyce said.

"Who should have been with Elizabeth, Joyce?" The King himself raised Rex to his feet, and the boy looked around him dazedly.

"Ruth Leslie. I cannot think where she can be."

Morton came back. "There is but one guardsman on duty, my liege. I found him at the other gate. Two men at work saw the boat start citywards. Of course they have no idea who was in it. Mistress Ruth, they say, was called away by her cousin, Sir Nicholas, and the Princess gave her leave to go."

"The kidnappers have not had much start. Come, Joyce and you also, Rex Damory. We must sift this to the bottom." With swift steps he re-entered the Tower, giving stern orders to the attendants as he went. He turned into his own private audience chamber.

"Now, Rex," he began, "what is all this about? Is this a Red Rose plot? What now, Richard?" as the Duke of Gloucester entered hastily.

"There is a rumor that Elizabeth has been captured by the Red Rose, Brother. This young rebel is at the bottom of the plot."

"What proof have you of this?"

"Ruth Leslie saw him in close converse with a Red Rose messenger not an hour agone."

Rex tried to speak, but the King held up a warning hand. "Silence, Rex Damory. This rumor seems to be true, Richard. Go and gather a guard. Seek Lord Dacre; threaten arrest if necessary and summon him and Lord Medanham to me."

Somewhat nonplussed, Duke Richard left. The King turned to Rex. "Sit down, boy. That was a shrewd blow. You are scarce in condition for questions as yet, even if you would answer them," he said. "You perilled yourself for the Princess and we will see to the blame of the matter later on."

A page entered and stood bowing low. The King looked at him.

"A traveller who refuses to give his name desires speech with Your Grace. He says his errand is of importance. Shall I admit him?"

"At once." Edward was ever unconventional in his direct dealing with his people, and even his own anxiety counted for nothing here, "Bring him in, Gilbert. Wait, Joyce, for I have somewhat more to say to you."

The stranger came in, but at the sight of him, Rex grew pale.

"What do you desire?" asked the King.

"I have come to surrender to you, my lord."

"O Rance, Rance," broke from Rex as the cloak was flung back, and the squire stood revealed. "Why have you done this?"

"I feared you might have to take the blame of this plot, my young lord. I have only just found out Sir Nicholas Leslie has a hand in this."

"Is this the squire of whom you told me, Rex Damory?" asked the King.

"Aye, my lord. It is Rance."

"You were head of the defence at Damory Court?"

"I was, lord King."

"Like the boy, I must ask why you have come?"

"After Damory's fall, I fled to France, lord King. Then, when this new plot started, I ventured back to England to take service with our folk. A man, Forrest by name, told us that my young lord here would be eager and able to help us, and I was sent to gain admittance. It was easier than I thought. The place was practically unguarded. I was not to tell the whole plot, but to find out from lord Rex just when the Princess Elizabeth would walk in the pleasance. I ought to have known him better. He refused to break his word. Then when I got back, I found that the plot had fallen through, and, moreover, the man Forrest belonged to my lord of Gloucester's troop and was the special attendant of Sir Nicholas Leslie. I knew his hate of Damory of old to my cost."

"What was the plot?"

"To seize the Princess; wed her to my lord Henry and hold her hostage for his safety and others of the Red Rose lords."

"A wild scheme indeed, with Henry Tudor a semi-prisoner and negotiations taking place to deliver him into our hands!"

"Desperate men use desperate measures, my lord. Perchance these very negotiations gave rise to the plot."

"Where is the Princess now?"

"Did they seize her after all? It will do them little good. My young lord of Fortescue has arrived, and he says that the Earl of Richmond will wed no unwilling bride and that the Red Rose does not war on maids."

"Do you own yourself to have plotted against me, Rance?"

"Aye, my lord."

"That dooms you then. But the sentence can bide. You must go to close ward. Say your farewells to the boy."

"Rance, Rance." Rex sprang forward eagerly.

"Mine own dear lord."

He would have bent his knee, but Rex flung his arms about him, and the old squire held him close. Then he released him.

"Grieve not for me, lad. All is well if you are safe."

"Come, Rance." The King's guard had entered, and Joyce came forward to lay her hand on Rex's arm. The squire started.

"Who are you, mistress?"

"Joyce Deventry." She looked at him in surprise.

"Methinks if likeness speak, your lost is found, lord Rex. The maid has the look of Lady Elsie."

"She is kin to the Leslies."

"What does that mean?" asked the King.

"Sir Nicholas Leslie carried off my twin sister Ruth after the siege of Damory, eight years agone, my lord. Rance thinks Joyce might be she."

"Your sister? Oh, that it might be, Rex!" Joyce cried. "But Sir Nicholas will never speak, and how can we find out if this is true?"

"You can find out nothing now," said the King sternly. "Go, Rance."

With a bow the squire obeyed. The King turned to the boy and girl. "Joyce, you must return to the Princess Elizabeth's apartments," he said. "You, Rex Damory, go to Prince Edward and hold yourself in close arrest until this matter is ended. I must take further means to seek for the Princess."

"The Princess is below, lord King." Another page had entered. The King sprang to his feet.

"Bring her hither instantly," he cried.

A moment later, she ran into his arms. Behind her came one at sight of whom Rex's eyes grew wide, for it was none other than John Fortescue himself.

"How did you come back to me, Bess?" asked the King.

"Forrest and another man came into the garden and carried me off. I found myself at last in the presence of two stern men who told me I was hostage for the Red Rose and that I should be sent to Brittany and there wedded to Prince Henry. I refused, and things were like to go hard with me, when my lord here came to my aid. Royal Father, you will not harm him who has perilled himself for me?"

"God forbid it, Bess." He turned to her escort. "What? John Fortescue!"

"Aye, Your Grace." The young lord bowed low. "I have brought back your daughter."

"And perilled yourself, you obstinate young rebel. There is a price upon your head only less than that upon Richmond's."

"I trust to you, lord King." John Fortescue smiled.

"I shall not abuse the trust. Get you gone. In three days' time, the hue and cry must be upon your heels. But you should be safe in France by then."

"I thank Your Grace." He would have gone, but Elizabeth ran forward.

"I thank you, my lord," she said shyly. "I was sore afraid and you helped me."

"Which was reward enough, little Princess."

"Are all Red Rose rebels alike?" asked the King. "This lad here risks his life for his plighted word, and you, my lord, might have won safety and a royal bride for your Prince."

"Whom yet he may come a-wooing," said John quietly. "The Red Rose has not yet fallen so low that it wars on maids, Your Grace."

"I owe you great thanks, nevertheless," said the King. He summoned a page. "Go, call Morton hither," he ordered.

John Fortescue spoke bluntly. "There is one warning that I would give Your Grace. Your chief danger lies not from us or from our broken Cause. There is peril nearer home. Guard well your lads and your maids. Moreover, if I be permitted the suggestion, your sons are safer apart. Two fatal accidents are not like to happen at once in London and in Wales."

"Whom do you accuse?"

"None in words, Your Grace, but I know whereof I speak."

The King drew his brows together in a frown. Morton entered.

"Take my lord Fortescue in safety to the coast, Morton," the King commanded. "Rex Damory, go back to the Prince. Bess, take your maiden Joyce and bide with your lady mother for the present."

Marvelling at the strange chances which had befallen him but with his heart heavy for Rance, Rex obeyed. He passed Ruth in the courtyard, and she flung back her head disdainfully as she passed him.

"Your day is coming, Red Rose rebel," she said.

"You may overreach yourself, proud girl," Rex retorted. "Why did you not bide with your Princess?"

"It is none of your affair—" she began, but Rex passed on to be greeted by the young Prince, who was consumed with curiosity over his absence.

"It was an errand which took me to your royal father," Rex told him. "Your sister is safe and will be with the Queen tonight."

It was not until late the next morning that Nicholas Leslie appeared with the summons to the King.

"You are to come at once," he told Rex curtly. "Prince Edward, the King summons you also to the court."

The two boys obeyed the call and entered the great court room to find a formal and formidable assembly. The King sat at the great table with Duke Richard at his right hand. He motioned to Edward to take the seat at the left. Rex stood before him.

The King spoke calmly. "Rex Damory, the Duke of Gloucester brings a serious charge against you, that of breaking your plighted word and conspiring with the Red Rose to kidnap the Princess Elizabeth."

"And also of abetting the escape of John Fortescue, even if he did not wholly compass it," interrupted the Duke. "This dangerous young rebel is known to have been within the Tower precincts. Yet when I came to arrest him, he was gone."

"What have you to say, Rex Damory?" In spite of his grave tone there was amusement in the King's keen eyes.

"That I have kept my word, Your Grace."

"Have you any witness to bring, my lord of Gloucester?"

"Mistress Ruth Leslie."

"Call her."

She came in, demure enough in appearance, though her lip curled as she caught sight of Rex.

"Ruth," said the King, "the Duke of Gloucester says that you have proof that Rex Damory has had speech with Red Rose rebels."

"He has, Your Grace. Yestermorn, I followed him down to the courtyard where one stood waiting for him. Sir Nicholas Leslie had suspected that he would try to meet the Red Rose adherents, and he bade me keep watch. I hid in the inner chamber that has a window opening on the court. I heard him greet the man as Rance."

"How had this man gained admittance?"

"I know not, Sire."

"Rex Damory did not admit him?"

"Nay, Sire, for the guard had summoned him."

"Was there but one guard there?"

"Only one that day."

"Are there not usually five or six, my lord of Gloucester?"

Richard flushed uneasily. "I was short of men for the outer barbican, Brother, and therefore withdrew them."

"Strange that on that particular day, the Red Rose rebels should know it."

"Rex Damory knew."

"Did he leave the Tower, my son?" The King turned to the Prince.

"No, royal Father."

"Did it not occur to you, Ruth, that your place was with the Princess?"

"I had been told that she was in danger from Rex Damory."

"Yet while you were absent, the attempt was made to carry her prisoner."

"I was told that she was with you, Sire."

"She was not."

"Brother, this Red Rose rebel knew of the plot." Duke Richard interposed. "Does he deny it?"

"No, he does not deny it," said the King. "Morton, fetch hither the Princess and Mistress Joyce Deventry. Also the prisoner, Rance."

"You have captured him?" gasped the Duke.

"He surrendered. Ah, there you are, Bess. Who carried you off?"

"A man named Forrest. I had seen him in my lord of Gloucester's troop. The rest I told you, my Father, and who saved me."

"Then sit down, little maid. Joyce, who told you of this plot?"

"Rex Damory, Your Grace. He came up from the courtyard. We went straight to the gardens. He attacked the man who was carrying away our Princess."

"Enough. Now, Rance, the squire, how did you know that the guard was reduced to one?"

"A man named FitzAllen told us, my lord. Afterwards I found it was a trap for my lord Rex, and I came then to Your Grace."

"Who was at the back of this?"

"To the best of my belief, Sir Nicholas Leslie. He has ever hated Damory and Damory's lord."

"Am I on trial?" asked Nicholas haughtily.

"Peace, Sir Nicholas. I wish to get to the bottom of this. It is common talk that you are no friend to Rex Damory. In what way has this enmity been shown, Rance?"

"It resulted in the death of my young lord's mother, Your Grace, though Sir Nicholas meant it not. He fought with Sir Hugh in the great hall of Damory and would have slain him but that my lady threw herself between. He hated Sir Hugh because of a quarrel in their boyhood. When my lady fell, he fled, but he took with him Rex Damory's twin sister in revenge."

"Where is the maid?"

"We know not. I have thought this might be the maid. She has a look of my lady."

"This passes bearing." Nicholas spoke icily. "I have suffered wrong enough from Damory without this despicable attempt to take my daughter from me."

"Yours? Oh, no! No! No!" Joyce cried, covering her face with shaking hands.

"Mine," said Nicholas calmly.

"We never heard that you were wedded, Sir Nicholas," said the King.

"I wedded a cousin of Elsie's a month after her marriage to Hugh Damory. My maid, Joyce, was born the same year as his son. The child was only six when she was left motherless. For my own reasons, I left her with a kinsman and brought her up as Joyce Deventry."

"And what of Sir Hugh Damory's daughter, Sir Nicholas? By my troth, Red Rose rebel as he was, had he brought his appeal to me, the maid would have been returned."

"She stands there." Nicholas Leslie pointed to Ruth.

Her face blazed; her eyes grew dark with wrath. "You lie, you lie!" she cried furiously. "I am a Leslie and a White Rose maid."

Rex looked at her aghast. She caught his glance and stamped her foot in a rage.

"I will not own you," she cried. "O Sire, Sire, you will not link me with the Red Rose rebel?"

"You are hard indeed, Ruth," said the King gravely. "Yet the blame is not so much yours as his who took so scurvy a vengeance. Nicholas Leslie, I take this matter into my own hands. These maids are wards of the crown, their estates in chancery. Elizabeth, go to your apartments and take both of them with you."

The girls obeyed. The King turned as Duke Richard came forward.

"All this has not disproven my charge against Rex Damory, Brother. There is only the word of a pack of maids that he did not take part in this plot."

"I can disprove it myself, Richard." The King spoke with stern emphasis. "Rex Damory risked his life for Elizabeth, and I myself saw it. He kept his plighted word at bitter cost."

"That does not prove the other issue. Do you realize that young rebel, Fortescue, was here in this very Tower and escaped?"

"You insist upon pressing this charge?"

"Is it not a serious one?"

"Truly."

"Then I press it."

"The culprit must confess then. Rex Damory had nothing to do with John Fortescue's escape. I arranged for it and sent him to the coast myself."

"Were you mad?"

"I trust not. White Rose folk do not war on those who succor their maids, Richard. John Fortescue risked life and liberty for Elizabeth, and I let him go and aided him."

"Then I apologize, Rex Damory." Never had the Duke seemed franker or more friendly than when he held out his hand.

"I thank Your Grace," Rex was forced to say as he accepted it.

"I have a mission for you, Richard," said the King. "There is trouble in the Scotch marches which needs a strong hand and a keen eye. Take command there."

"You would have me leave you, Brother, when you are ill?" asked the Duke suavely.

"For the sake of the kingdom, aye. Be ready to start with tomorrow's dawn."

"Richard ever obeys his King." The Duke bent and kissed the King's hand, but the stern gaze bent upon him did not relax. He left the room, followed by Nicholas.

"Rance," said the King, "I know your love of your young lord. For his sake will you take allegiance to me?"

"Nay, Your Grace. Such service would do you little good. How could you trust one who had forsaken an exiled Prince and his master's Cause?"

"I judged that you would answer thus. Well, I am considered harsh. The Red Rose terms me a relentless foe, but never yet has Edward of England taken the life of one who trusted him. You must go into exile as you have been these past eight months. Bid the boy farewell. Morton will speed you on your way."

"Allegiance I may not give you, my lord Edward, but you are safe from plot of mine," Rance answered sturdily. "For eight long months you have protected my young lord, a greater boon to me than my own liberty." He bent and kissed Rex's hand. "God keep you, my young lord," he said, and followed Morton from the room.

"I thank Your Grace for this," Rex said, raising grateful eyes to the King.

"The thanks are still on my side. You have served me and mine right well. The Red Rose rebel is more loyal than the sworn liegeman, methinks. Now, go to Edward. I fear you have your own problems to solve, lad, for your newfound sister does not take kindly to this discovery of her lineage. But there is another side to Ruth. Win her."

VII

Prisoners

"WHAT AM I to do, Rex?" Joyce asked despairingly the next day, as she walked with him along the river bank. "I cannot even respect, much less love, my father. Truly, the future is black indeed."

Rex looked at her anxiously. There were dark shadows under her eyes which told of a sleepless night. Her face was colorless, and, for the time, the steadfast courage which was characteristic of her had been crushed out by this unexpected blow.

"Grieve not, Joyce," he said in an effort to comfort her. "After all, the King has taken over your guardianship, and Nicholas Leslie can trouble you but little."

She shivered. "If you could have seen his face when he bade me farewell, Rex, you would not wonder at my fears. 'Make the most of your time, girl,' he said, and his smile of evil satisfaction has haunted me ever since."

"You are overwrought or you would not be borrowing trouble like this," Rex said. "The King is powerful and Princess

Elizabeth loves you, Joyce."

"I am troubling you with my worries when you have your own," she said penitently. "How are you progressing with Ruth?"

Rex laughed ruefully. "I am going backwards, Joyce. Ruth hated me as Red Rose rebel, but that is a mere nothing to her vindictive dislike of me now. The King bade me win her, but how am I to win a maid who alternates periods of stony silence with violent threats on my life? The only thing I can do is to wait till something like reason comes to her aid. Sir Nicholas, in this respect, won in his vengeance on Damory. Thank the Lord, my father did not encounter it. Ruth's hate would have broken his heart."

"We will fight it out together, Rex. Here comes Morton. I wonder what he wants."

The tall guardsman came up. "The King would have you ready to start with Prince Edward for Cardiff within the hour, my lord. The King would speak with you now."

With a brief farewell to Joyce, Rex made his way to the royal apartments. The King lay back wearily in his great chair. His illness was heavy upon him, and his face was gray and drawn with pain. But he spoke with his usual stern self-control.

"Rex, I am sending Edward to his uncle, Lord Rivers, at Cardiff. You will accompany him, and there he will remain for the present. The two lads are safer apart. I trust you, boy."

The door was flung open, and Edward with little Duke Richard came in. The older boy came straight to his father's side.

"Why do you send me away, royal Father?" he asked.

"For your own safety, my son. If God spares me to make new plans, you shall return to me before long. But since you and Richard have been together, we have lived in a seething pot of plot and counterplot."

"I like not to leave you so ill, my Father."

"But Edward of Wales will obey his King." The sick monarch

drew the boy close. "Lad, you are old enough to know that I am sick unto death. Please God, we may yet meet again, but if not, remember that I leave you the trust of England. May God protect and strengthen you, my son."

He kissed the boy on the brow. Edward clung to him. "God grant that I be such a King as you," he whispered.

"A better one I trust." The King laid his hand on the boy's head. "Weep not, Edward. We be Plantagenets, and Plantagenets bear the lion's heart. Now go." He drew Richard to his side. "You shall bide with me, my little lad."

He watched Edward as he went, head erect and with a smile for his father though the hand which held Rex's was cold and trembling. In an hour they were on their way, and two days later, Lord Rivers welcomed them to Cardiff.

THE WEEKS that followed were pleasant for both lads. In spite of his anxiety, Edward found that the new freedom was one over which to rejoice. The two scrambled over the cliffs or spent long hours on the water, while Edward's laugh rang out as merrily as Rex's own, and the color came back into a face which had grown pale and worn under the stress and confinement of court life. Their friendship grew each day, and in this new companionship, Rex forgot the heartache which Ruth's hate had caused him.

But one day as they came in to their nooning, it was to see the grave figure of Lord Woodville awaiting them. One glance at his face told Rex the tidings that he bore, but Edward ran forward eagerly.

"What news of my father, Uncle?"

"There is heavy tidings for Your Grace," Lord Woodville answered and Edward's eyes grew frightened, as he realized what the formality of the address must mean.

"My father is worse?" he asked anxiously.

"He rests at last, Edward. There was no time to fetch you, the end came so suddenly. He sent you his love and blessing and bade you be brave as a king should be."

The boy stood looking at him dazedly for a few moments, then he flung himself down on the couch, his whole frame shaken with sobs while Rex stood by with Lord Woodville, helpless to comfort him.

"Talk to him, Rex," Lord Woodville said at last, and Rex knelt down beside him and put his arm lovingly about the young King. Edward returned the embrace and strove to regain his composure.

"My father, my father, how can I do without him? I want to be brave but I want him so."

Lord Rivers came into the room hastily and went to his side. "You will not fail him, Edward," he said gently and, putting his arm about the boy, drew him close. He said no more but let that first passionate grief spend itself. Then, as the boy grew quieter, he spoke tenderly, yet gravely, too.

"You must cease your weeping, Edward. A King cannot stay to indulge his grief. We must start for London as swiftly as may be. Your father looked to you to be a royal Plantagenet."

"I will keep trust." Lord Rivers' own eyes filled as he saw the gallant fight for self-control. Then he knelt and did homage. Lord Grey and Lord Woodville did likewise.

"We, with a council of safety, are left your guardians, my liege," Lord Woodville said.

"With my uncle of Gloucester?" Edward asked.

"He was sent to take command in the Scotch marches and was mentioned not. Rex Damory, go aid your young King to make ready: we will start within the hour."

It was well within that time when they started out, riding on swiftly, and sheltering for the night at Glastonbury. All went well till they came to Stony Stratford the next day, when some difficulty in changing horses caused a delay. They were just remounting when a messenger rode posthaste to Lord Rivers, who stood near the boy King.

"His Grace of Gloucester sends greeting, my lord," he said. "He asks that you, Lord Grey, and Lord Woodville, meet him at Nottingham where he waits."

Lord Grey uttered an exclamation of annoyance. "Methought he was in Scotland. By bright Saint George, he travels as fast as bad news."

"He is bad news," said Edward quaintly.

"Well, there is naught to do but ride on and meet him," Lord Grey decided. "My liege, you had best bide here for an hour and then ride on to meet us."

With a few attendants, they set spurs to their horses and Edward re-entered the inn. "Mark my words, Rex, he will have made himself Lord Protector by this time," he said.

"How could he, my lord?"

"He will have his way by fair means or foul," Edward insisted. "There is trouble ahead, Rex."

An hour later, they set forth, but they had hardly left Stratford when they saw Duke Richard approaching.

Edward stood under a giant oak, his head thrown back, his slight boyish figure drawn to its full height. Rex stood near, holding his horse, while just behind were Sir Richard Hause and Sir Thomas Vaughan, the young King's favorite attendants.

Richard of Gloucester bent his knee with ready grace.

"Edward of England, I am your liegeman and do you homage for my manors of Gloucester and Nevelle," he said, then rising, took him in his arms. "Poor fatherless lad, yours is a sore loss.

But weep not, Edward, you shall find a father in me, unworthy
though I be to take his place."

"I thank you, fair uncle," Edward answered gravely.

"We must resume our journey at once," the Duke continued.
"I would see you lodged comfortably, Edward, for I am now
responsible for your safety, since Parliament has named me Lord
Protector."

"Methought Lord Grey and Lord Rivers were my guardians,"
Edward objected. "My father desired that."

"Parliament decides such matters, sweet nephew."

"And I submit to the law of the realm," answered the boy.
"But where are my uncles? Why did they not come back with
you?"

"Dear lad, how shall I tell you? I hoped you would not miss
them yet. Your father is not cold in his grave, and Lord Grey and
Lord Rivers have plotted against you. By order of Parliament, I
have put them under arrest and sent them to Pontefract."

The color died out of Edward's face. Only too well he knew
that few who reached the grim fortress ever came back. "It is
a base plot," he cried. "They are true and I know it. Where is
Lord Woodville?"

"I trust he will clear himself of complicity, boy. I have sent
him to London." The Duke cast his eyes over the horror-stricken
assembly. "I see two others implicated in this foul conspiracy.
Buckingham, take under arrest Sir Thomas Vaughan and Sir
Richard Hause."

The Duke of Buckingham stepped forward; the young
King clung to his doomed servants but, relentlessly, they were
marched away.

"Rex Damory, you also are implicated," Richard began, but
Edward had recovered himself. His lips set resolutely.

"This passes bearing, my lord of Gloucester. Rex Damory quits
not my side. He is attached to my person, and I say he shall not go."

"I am Lord Protector, Edward, and you cannot prevent it."

"I can and will prevent it, my uncle. If you force my lord of
Damory from me, I will proclaim your deeds in every town and
village we pass nor will I enter London save as a prisoner bound
and gagged; and that, my lord of Gloucester, you dare not do—
yet."

Richard looked nonplussed, for Edward was right. He gazed
blankly at him for a moment, then recovered himself with an
effort.

"I have your best interests at heart, sweet nephew. I fear you
will repent your gracious clemency to this Red Rose rebel, but
Rex Damory shall go with you." He smiled winningly again as he
spoke, but the hate that shot from his eyes made Rex say again
the King's sorrowful words, "There is trouble ahead."

The dreariness of that ride and the long wakeful night when
the boy King lay sobbing in his arms was one Rex never forgot.
Early in the morning they were on their way again and rode on
with heavy hearts through the crowds of cheering populace.
At Huntley, the Lord Mayor and four hundred citizens met
them. There was a long speech of welcome, at the end of which
a messenger, splashed with the mud and mire of hard travel,
rode up to the Protector. There was a whispered conversation of
which the only words audible were "The Queen." Edward rode
forward.

"What news of my lady mother?" he asked imperiously.

"Naught of importance, save that she has taken sanctuary
with your brother," answered the Duke with darkening face.

"Then he is safe, thank the Lord," said Edward.

It was late in the afternoon when they reached London. The
weary boys saw with relief the gray walls of the Bishop's palace.
There they rested, but only for an hour. Before the evening meal
was finished, the Duke entered.

"Come, sweet nephew, I will take you to your brother."

"In sanctuary, my uncle?"

"Of course not. I soon persuaded your fair mother out of her foolishness. Richard is in the state apartments of the Tower."

"I like not the Tower," Edward objected.

"It is the safest place, dear lad. London is in such a turmoil that I fear for you at present. Rex goes with you, and with Morton as guard, you need not worry. God grant that some day, Edward, you will learn to trust me, and to believe that I have your welfare at heart."

"I will go," Edward said wearily.

It was in the dusk of the long June evening that they approached the Tower. Suddenly a group of horsemen rode towards them and Edward, with a cry of joy, recognized the lady they were guarding.

"O Mother, sweet Mother," he cried.

Elizabeth threw back her heavy veil and clasped him in her arms. "My son, my son," she sobbed.

"I feared I might not see you again, Mother. Are you to accompany us?"

"Alas, no. I go to Castle York and he, whom I dread most of all men, holds my chiefest treasures."

"Rex will be with us, sweet Mother."

"Aye. Rex, you will care for my boys?"

"As my own life, sweet lady."

The Duke rode up. "Come, Edward, we must hasten. The night comes on apace."

Again and again, the young King kissed his mother, the tears springing to his eyes, bravely as he fought to keep them back.

"Fare you well, Edward. The God of the fatherless protect you and bring you to your own. Guard him well, Rex." She laid Edward's hand in his friend's.

"My life is his," Rex answered, and the Queen turned to the Duke. She spoke with solemn emphasis.

111

"God do to you and yours, Richard Gloucester, as you do to my fatherless boys," she said. For a moment, the Duke's face whitened, then he laid his hand on Edward's bridle rein.

"You pass the bounds of courtesy, my Lady Elizabeth," he answered icily. "Get you gone to Castle York; I see where the boy has learned his unreasonable hatred. Come, Edward." The procession passed on within the grim precincts of the Tower.

"I pray you, Uncle, may I not see my sister?" Edward asked, as little Duke Richard clung to him in eager greeting. The Protector hesitated.

"She will join your mother at Castle York and will set forth with the dawning," he said doubtfully. "I will send her to you this evening."

"I thank you, my lord." Edward spoke gratefully and a few moments later they were left alone.

The apartments were not their old ones but those of the King. Edward's eyes filled more than once as he looked around at the familiar things, the King's favorite chair, the Queen's tapestry stool, the tiny objects which spoke to him of his loss. But he did not give way. Suddenly, there came the sound of light footsteps, and the door opened to admit Princess Elizabeth and Joyce. For a moment the royal children clung together, sobbing in their grief, then Elizabeth regained her self-control. She glanced at Rex.

"You may go yonder and speak with Rex Damory, Joyce," she said, and Ruth, entering the room at the moment, frowned at the words. She did not, however, dare to join them. She stood at the doorway casting vindictive looks upon her brother. Joyce and he stood at the great embrasure looking out on the Tower garden.

"Do you go with the Princess and our lady Queen to Castle York?" Rex said.

"I think so, though Ruth is not to go. I believe she is to go to

Devonshire. Rex, is all well with you? My heart misgave me when I heard of the arrests."

"I were in prison tonight but for the King." Rex looked over at Edward. "How long he can protect me I cannot say, but methinks it will be but a short time. My lord of Gloucester does not forget."

"Can you not escape to France? The King would let you go at the hint of danger."

"Truth to tell, Joyce, his danger is no less than mine. I could not leave him while there is a chance to protect him. But what of yourself, Joyce? Are you safe?"

"I know not." She shook her sunny head. "My father seems to hate me worse than ever. O Rex, there be times when life seems over hard."

"Truly. Yet, Joyce, as we rode hither, I had a chance to fight the battle out. I used to dream in those old days at Damory of valiant deeds such as my forebears did of old, of perchance falling in defence of country and King. Yet now I see this is my battle-field and all I have to do is to stand like the old crusader did, doing my duty and trusting my life to God. Please Him, if I die, it shall be true to my trust."

Her face flushed as he spoke. "I will do likewise, Rex. If this be my sore battle-field, I too will stand, I will keep trust and do my duty even to the father who likes me not."

"We must go, Joyce." Princess Elizabeth came up to them. She held out her hand to Rex.

"I fear your peril is not over, Rex Damory, but it is a comfort to know that you are with him and will guard him well."

Rex bent and kissed her hand. "I will do my best, sweet lady," he said, and with her eyes on her brother's face, her arm about Joyce, Elizabeth withdrew. Rex turned to his sister.

"May I speak with you, Ruth?" he asked.

"A Red Rose rebel can have naught to say which interests me," she retorted.

"Perhaps not. This thing which has come upon us is as hard upon you as upon myself. Since I first heard of you, I dreamed of a sister, though I might have known that Nicholas Leslie would have taken care that the Ruth I found was naught but another foe. But I stand in the shadow of death today, and my chance for serving or troubling you will soon be at an end."

"You would like to shake me again?"

A gleam of amusement came into his eyes. "There would be satisfaction in it, I admit. But I am going to do nothing of the sort. After all, you are my sister, and when I die you are heir to Damory and our broad lands. You should lay claim to the manor for there is no entail."

"I shall turn it into a White Rose stronghold."

"That matters not. When one stands in the shadow of death, the wars of the rival Roses seem but little after all."

"Why do you think yourself in such dire peril?"

"I am in the hands of the two who hate me most. But for the King I should have been in prison tonight."

"You hate them just as much although you act in such a saint-like fashion."

Rex spoke grimly. "There is no saintliness in me today. If I could crush Nicholas Leslie, word or no word, I would do it now, aye, and his master with him."

She laughed. "You spoke like a Leslie then and not a puling Damory. I rouse the worst in you, Rex."

"Not you but this last wrong." He glanced over at the young King. "If I could save him—"

"You talk folly. He is in no danger, but if he were," her face softened strangely, "for once, I should stand beside you, Rex."

"You must go. Farewell and God keep you," Rex answered. He turned back to the King. Ruth stared after him for a moment, then with a little catch in her breath she sped after the Princess.

THE DAYS that followed were hard for all the boys: liberty
of walking in the enclosed garden was denied them and little
Richard began to pine under the close confinement. Edward
and Rex exerted themselves for his amusement. But, one after
the other, every employment palled. The Duke seldom came
near them, though they saw him from the window from time
to time seeking the council chamber. Of those at Castle York
they gained no tidings, save that once Father Oswald came to
wait upon the boy King, and to tell Rex that there was news that
Rance had reached Spain in safety and was in the field against
the Moors. No regular chaplain was appointed to the royal chapel, and the daily services which the boys attended were served by
different priests.

"We have been here more than six weeks, and I am aweary,
Rex," Edward said one day. "I see my uncle is in the council
chamber, and I am going to appeal in front of the council for
some small liberty. Come with me."

"You had best not anger him, my liege. It will do no good," Rex
urged. But the King went on his willful way. Down the long corridors and winding stairs the two lads passed, and as they reached
the council chamber, the sound of angry voices reached them.

"I swear I will not dine until I have your head." The voice was
Richard of Gloucester's.

"Come, Rex," and Edward, his face flushed with anger,
opened the door.

In the center of the room stood the Lord Protector, his eyes
flashing, his face crimson with passion, his lame arm bared, as
he confronted Lord Hastings, white-haired, but erect and daunt-

less despite his eighty years. He faced the angry Duke with calm contempt, as the guards pinioned him.

"Do your worst. I fear you not. Before the council I repeat my words," he challenged. "You are traitor, Richard of Gloucester, traitor to your nephew and to the realm of England."

"Take him to the courtyard this instant," Richard ordered.

"Touch him on your peril," cried a ringing, boyish voice, and Edward confronted his uncle.

"Edward, go instantly to your own apartments," ordered the Duke angrily.

"I will not, my lord. What has Lord Hastings done?"

"He has conspired against me."

"Folly, my Lord Protector," Edward blazed. "Traitor are you, as Lord Hastings terms you."

"Take Lord Hastings to the courtyard," ordered Richard curtly.

"Unhand him this instant," Edward told the guards.

"My liege," Lord Hastings said quietly, "I pray you let me go. You cannot save me, and the Lord Protector shortens my life by very little. Heaven bless and keep you, my King."

"Uncle, my uncle," Edward pleaded, as Lord Hastings stooped and kissed his hand and then suffered his executioners to lead him away.

"I have sworn that he shall die, Edward. Well is it for your lady mother that she is at Castle York!"

With a low cry of anguish, Edward turned away and none in all that august assembly dared face the anger of the Protector by showing sympathy. The guard came back.

"Lord Hastings is dead, Your Grace."

"So perish all traitors," returned the Duke solemnly; and Edward, growing deathly white, suffered Rex to lead him away. As the door closed behind them, they heard Richard address the council in suave tones.

"I pray you forgive this scene, my lords. Would that my duty suffered me to be gentler with yon poor lad. My action was for his safety far more than for my own. He has been taught to hate me. Truly the place I fill is one of agony, obliged to send to death my old-time comrades and to deal blow after blow on the tender heart of my brother's son." Rex glancing back saw him bow his head on his hands and caught the low sympathetic murmur, "Long live our Protector; God comfort Your Grace."

It was the worst of their days. Edward broke down completely, and Rex and little Richard were occupied in tending him. The climax came at sunset. Edward rose from his couch with a shiver as the familiar firm step of his uncle sounded in the corridor and Morton, bowing low, announced, "The Lord Protector, my liege."

The Duke seated himself and surveyed his nephew with stern eyes. "By what right dared you come to the Council chamber this morning?"

"Are we prisoners, my lord? I came but to ask a question. The Prince of Wales had a right to walk in one enclosed garden; the King of England lives a prisoner in the State apartments."

"And will continue to do so until he learns that minors do not rule England. But sign this paper."

"I shall not sign till I know what it is, my lord."

"Then since you insist on knowing what concerns you not, it is the death warrant of the traitor, Thomas Woodville."

"And you would make me sign it? Not though I share Lord Hastings' fate."

"You refuse to do my bidding, Edward? You forget that I am Protector, till you come to man's estate."

"I will not sign it, uncle."

"Then I must do it for you." He signed the paper.

Edward clutched at Rex's arm, and with a loving gesture the boy supported him. A sudden surge of anger came over him as the Duke laughed and Edward grew more white.

"Coward," Rex cried, forgetful of all save the King's agony. "How can you torment him thus? Oh, would that England knew!"

"Beware, Rex Damory." Richard spoke with deliberate cruelty. "Lord Grey and Lord Rivers died at Pontefract this morning; Lord Woodville dies tomorrow; for whom do you think the next death warrant will be?"

"My uncles, my uncles! I am all alone!" Edward cried and his fair head fell back senseless on Rex's shoulder. The boy laid him down, and turned in white anger on the Duke.

"Are you satisfied now, my lord?" he asked indignantly.

"I have a heavy score to settle with you, Rex Damory," was the Duke's answer as he left the room.

Rex did not heed him as he knelt beside the King.

It was long before he recovered, and Rex was obliged to summon Morton to aid. At last the boy stirred, sighed and came to his senses with a burst of grief.

"Have I killed him, Rex? What shall I do? Will he believe the falsehood?"

"Nay, nay, my King, he knows you far too well."

"What has happened?" Morton asked and, briefly, Rex told the tale. The man pondered. "I could take you to my Lord Woodville, Lord Rex," he said.

"I fear to leave the King," Rex objected.

"Go, Rex," Edward urged with brightening face.

"Go, tell him how it is I cannot save him. Tell him—oh, nothing can blot it out—tell him what you will."

With heavy heart, Rex obeyed. A few moments later he found himself in Lord Woodville's prison.

"Now can I learn the truth, dear lad," the prisoner said. "Does Edward count me guilty and demand immediate death?"

"We feared that lie was told you. The King is breaking his

heart because he cannot save you. It is all a plot, my lord, the intrigue of his Grace of Gloucester."

"As I had guessed." Lord Woodville spoke steadfastly. "Now can I die in peace, though my heart misgives me for the King. Bid him not grieve, but take courage and be patient for his brother's sake and for England. You will have to keep good watch, Rex. But you are loyal, I know."

"While I live, but I am doomed, my lord. The Duke practically told me that tonight."

"You, like the rest, have fallen under the blight of Richard's vengeance. God keep and help you, lad. Yet I know whatever may befall you, your courage will not fail. Here comes Morton. Farewell, Rex." He held the boy for a moment in a close embrace, then stood smiling as the door closed upon him.

The knell in the dawn found them waiting and the three boys knelt together. Rex looked in wonder at Edward's peaceful eyes. His face was pale and drawn with suffering, yet he made no moan as he prayed earnestly for the gallant soul which was passing for his sake. As the bell ceased, he drew little Richard close. "Weep not, little Brother. God will give us strength, and we must bear all things like royal Plantagenets."

The sound of approaching footsteps brought them all to their feet, and Edward advanced to meet the Lord Protector.

"Your Grace's will is done; Lord Woodville is dead," said Richard coolly.

Edward showed neither terror nor dismay. "If your will is accomplished and you have finished tormenting us, my lord Gloucester, we would be alone," he said, and, stung by his words, the haughty Duke turned and left him.

The day seemed endless, but it drew to a close at last, and the three sat in the window embrasure looking out on the green where they had been wont to play quoits and other games. The sun was setting over the water in a glow of crimson glory, and the faint gleam of the evening star could be seen in the twilight sky. Morton was off duty, and the sharp challenge of his substitute was answered by a rustle of paper. Then the door was pushed open, and the three turned with some apprehension as two masked men entered.

"What means this?" questioned the King.

"The Lord Protector has bidden us move you to other quarters," one man answered roughly.

"As the Lord Protector wills," Edward said quietly, and with his arm about his brother and Rex at his side, he followed the men.

Down the stairs of the State apartments they were led; out across the green to the Round Tower where prisoners of the crown were wont to be confined. Edward hesitated a moment as the great door was swung wide and the guard stood aside to let them climb the steep stairs, then he went on. Protests were useless, they all knew well.

They went up to find at the top a sort of double apartment, a sleeping chamber, ready furnished, and a larger room with table, stools, and chairs. The windows were heavily barred, and from down below came the swish of the Thames. The masked men saw them in, then the bolts shot home, and the three boys stood facing the fact that they were prisoners.

"Edward, Edward, what will become of us?" little Richard cried. "I like not this place. I am afraid."

"Plantagenets are not afraid," Edward answered cheerily. "Mayhap there is rioting in London and we be safer here, but if not, remember we be sons of a King and that our father was never afraid."

"I will remember." Richard choked back a sob. "But it is so like a prison, Edward."

Edward smiled. "And if it is so, we will play a new game tomorrow, Richard. We can do the Lionheart and Saladin and

120

many a knightly story."

The younger boy clapped his hands. "Then I am glad we came. We were never able to pretend aright before. Shall we be Knights Templar at Jerusalem, tomorrow?"

"Tonight if you will, Brother. Now Rex and I will help you to bed, for you must be ready when the test comes."

"Aye," said Richard. "We will keep faith when the Moors come, Edward?"

"We will keep faith always," Edward told him and Richard was comforted. He soon fell asleep. Edward beckoned Rex into the adjoining room.

"What do you think this means, Rex?"

Rex shook his head. "I know not, my King, unless belike London has risen for you. That would mean imprisonment for us all."

Edward's face went white. "It would mean death, Rex."

"Perchance, yet if it does, the strength will come for us both, my King. Remember your own brave words and be not afraid."

"I will try. I must not frighten Richard. You will help me, Rex?"

"To the utmost, my King."

But in spite of courage and patience, the days lagged on. Once Father Oswald contrived to come to them and reported that disturbances had taken place in the city and the Protector was at Warwick. Rex, though he said little to Edward, felt sure that his own fate was sealed, for Richard of Gloucester was not one to forget, even without the constant prod of Nicholas Leslie's hate. Then, Little Richard fell ill and as one hot stifling day succeeded another, his condition began to alarm his boy companions.

One hot afternoon when he had fallen into a heavy sleep, the two older lads stood together at the window and caught the sound of crowds along the river bank. Then suddenly the low surging murmur broke in a shout, "Long live our Protector,

Richard, Richard the Good!"

"Richard the Good," Edward repeated bitterly, then started and turned as the door opened and Nicholas Leslie entered.

"What do you here?" he asked.

"I bear His Grace of Gloucester's warrant." Nicholas came forward and laid his hand on his kinsman's shoulder. "Rex Damory, I arrest you, in the name of the King, on a charge of high treason."

"O Rex, Rex, it has come!" Edward threw himself between. "Sir Nicholas Leslie, I, the King, command you to unhand him."

"You cannot shield him now, Your Grace," Nicholas said sternly. "Come, Rex Damory."

"He shall not go!" Edward insisted.

"Then I shall fetch my lord of Gloucester."

"As you will," Edward defied him.

Nicholas went outside. "Go, tell the Duke of Gloucester that the King and Rex Damory resist his warrant," he said to the guard he had brought with him.

"I resist it not," Rex said quietly. "I surrender myself. Nay, my liege," as Edward caught his arm. "It is useless to fight this arrest; we have known this must be the end."

"It shall not be," Edward cried passionately. "Go, Sir Nicholas, ask my uncle to come hither."

Nicholas retired and Edward caught his friend's hands. "Rex, Rex must you too be sacrificed? Can his ambition leave not one?"

"Right willingly I die for you, my King, only I pray you anger not the Duke for my sake. Your kingdom, mayhap your own life, is at stake; what do I matter in comparison with you?"

"If aught can save you, Rex, you shall be saved." Edward stood in front of his friend while footsteps approached as Rex, outwardly calm but with fast beating heart, strove to resign himself to the inevitable end. The Duke entered.

"What means this, my lord of Gloucester?" Edward asked. "Why is my personal attendant arrested on a false charge of treason?"

"Your Grace is a minor and understands not the affairs of state."

"Then how does Rex Damory menace them? He is a minor too."

"He is a Red Rose rebel, steeped in intrigue, who was in league with those deep-dyed traitors, Grey and Woodville."

"What was this treachery?" Edward asked. "I have heard much of it, and for it my staunchest friends have died, yet it is never clear what the plot was. It is all a fabrication of yours, my lord, deny it if you can."

"Plot or no plot, you have no power in this, Edward. Rex Damory must die. He has interfered—"

"With your schemes." Edward clenched his hands. "He is too true and too loyal to me, and so he must die. You do not care, you who aim at a crown. What is a life to you? But you shall not have Rex. I am the King; I will protect him."

"Long live our Protector Richard, Richard the Good!" The shout of the crowd rang out again. The Duke smiled in cruel triumph.

"Hear you that, Edward? I am Protector. England bows to my will, and I say that Rex Damory must die."

Rex came forward. "Let us end this," he said firmly. "Say no more, my liege."

"Nay, Rex, I cannot let you go. Take not my last comfort. Spare me Rex." For a moment the Duke's face softened, and Edward caught his hand. "Have mercy, my uncle, hear me just this once."

But Richard's eyes grew hard again. "Peace, Edward," he said sternly. "I have spoken. Rex Damory must die."

The King turned a white agonized face to Rex. The boy came

to the Duke. "I yield myself to your will, my lord," he said, then turned to the King.

"Grieve not, my liege. I fear not to die for you seeing I have your love and trust. I thank you for your comradeship." He bent his knee and laid his hands in the King's in the attitude of homage. The Duke strode forward as if to interfere but something in Edward's face stopped him.

"Edward of England, I vow myself your liegeman unto my life's end," he said.

And the King, stooping, kissed his brow. "Farewell, Rex. We shall meet soon, for I know well that you alone stand between me and death."

"I am ready." Rex rose to his feet and held out his wrists to Nicholas, who fastened the chains upon them.

"I will spare you the ignominy of a public execution, Rex Damory," said the Duke. "It will take place tomorrow morn within the Tower walls."

"Tomorrow morn shall find me ready," Rex answered. "May I ask the boon of a priest tonight, Your Grace?"

"I will send you one," said the Duke, and Rex allowed Nicholas to lead him away, only turning once to smile at Edward.

"God keep you, Rex." The King's voice was steady now, as if his friend's courage had brought back his own. The door closed, and he stood facing his uncle.

"Long live our Protector Richard, Richard the Good!" came from the surging crowd along the river bank. "Long live Richard of Gloucester, Richard the Good!"

"God grant that England may never know the mercy and justice of Richard the Good," said the boy.

The Duke started as if stung. "How dare you, Edward?" he cried.

"Peace, my lord of Gloucester. You can deceive me no more. I know it is my life that you seek. Take it when you will. Nay," as Richard would have spoken, "I am not angry nor frightened now. I can only pity you, for I know that the day will come, when you will wish that you had died a boy at Castle York. God keep England from your evil rule. Go now, my lord. I would be alone."

The haughty Duke obeyed him without a word. Edward stood listening to the shouting crowd, facing in his loneliness the terrors of an unknown fate.

"Poor England," sighed the boy. "God keep my kingdom and make me strong to the end."

In one of the dark cells of the Tower, Rex, too, was alone. He had changed in this past year, and there was now none of the fierce rebellion which had marked his first imprisonment. He sat on the stool by the rough table, his head buried on his folded arm, trying to rally his courage. The door was opened and closed, but he did not move, till a hand was laid on his shoulder and a voice said, "Rex, lad." He sprang to his feet to face Father Oswald.

"I have permission to visit you as a priest tonight. Morton was sent with word to me. What has happened, boy?"

"You know that, with the King and his brother, I have been practically a prisoner for over a month now," said Rex. "Today I was arrested and condemned to death by the Lord Protector himself."

"He was here this afternoon?"

"Else had I not been here."

"It is passing strange. He has been ill, confined to his room and seeing none for days at Warwick Castle. He was not able to return even when the great demonstration of loyalty was made in the city. There is a rumor of a plot to seize the Tower and bring out the King. Morton was in sore distress because he had been told to go to Castle York. Sir John Brackenbury, Lord Lieutenant of the Tower, is to command at Black Heath tonight."

"I trust the plot succeeds, Father Oswald. If I only knew the King was safe, I could face the rest more calmly. My heart misgives me for his safety."

"You have done well and served him faithfully, dear lad."

"I am a coward tonight, Father Oswald. My heart has failed me. It is hard to die like this."

"You are innocent, Rex. You will not be alone, for He who called you to a share of His own cross, will bide beside you to the end, to welcome you to that great rest beyond all fear and pain."

"But to die without resistance; to let them work their will on me; to be bound and helpless; to endure the loneliness and the shame."

"He, Who was bound and helpless, understands, lad. And is there shame, when you die for love of the King, your friend and comrade?"

"Aye, it is for Edward." Rex's face lighted up. "I was wrong, Father. Would I could prove my love by even greater suffering."

"*Greater love hath no man than this, that a man lay down his life for his friends,*" quoted Father Oswald. "Now, Rex, let us to our holy gear, for I have but an hour with you."

He obeyed. The tense strain had loosened, and when he rose after his absolution and Communion, his face was full of peace. The door was opened, and a guardsman looked in. He wore the livery of Duke Richard.

"You must come, for after this none may pass the Tower gates till after dawn," he said gruffly, and with a parting blessing to the boy, Father Oswald left him. Wearied, Rex flung himself upon the stone couch and was soon sleeping soundly.

He was roused by a rough shake and saw Nicholas Leslie bending over him. The first beam of the dawn was straggling through the small barred window. The boy grew pale but did not falter as he faced his kinsman.

"I am ready, Sir Nicholas," he said, and would have walked to the door, but Nicholas pushed him back.

"The Lord Protector would speak with you," he said curtly and left the prison as Richard entered, closing the door behind him.

"Well, my lord, how like you your new quarters?" asked Richard mockingly.

"It matters little where one's last night on Earth is spent, Your Grace."

"Dauntless as ever," Richard laughed. "Well, Rex Damory, I offer you your life."

"On what condition?"

"Perchance your youth has touched my heart and I give it to you unconditionally. Has not that occurred to you?"

"No." Rex met his eyes steadily. "I know full well, my lord of Gloucester, that your hate for me is such that my life could only be purchased from you at a cost which would make the gift unbearable."

Richard's face flushed. "'Troth, Rex Damory, they were right who term you brave. I know not another in England who would answer me thus."

"I stand in the shadow of death and fear is over, Your Grace."

"We shall see," said Richard grimly. "But you are right. There is a condition. The estates of the realm have this day chosen me for King in the place of my fair nephew."

"You blackhearted traitor!" Rex cried.

"Wait. This paper sets forth Edward's unfitness for the throne. If signed by you, his known companion, it will carry weight with those who else might whisper that I was over eager to seize the crown. Sign it, Rex Damory, and you are free."

"Never. I will be true to the King though it cost my life."

"Count that cost. Sign, and an earldom is yours, refuse and—"

"There is but death," Rex answered.

"No easy one shall be yours. Suffering and death—fear you not that, boy?"

Rex stood appalled by the awful choice. He clenched his hands as he strove to decide. Was it only a few hours ago he had longed to suffer more for the King?

"Well, Rex, an earldom or suffering? Your life or your allegiance?" Richard of Gloucester thought his victory won.

"My allegiance, Your Grace."

"Do you realize what this means? Do you yield your life to me?"

"For Edward's sake I yield it."

"We will prove you then." The Duke went to the door. "Nicholas, bring Forrest and FitzAllen," he called.

Nicholas Leslie entered, followed by the two men. They punished Rex to the point that he suffered as he never had before.

"Will you yield now, Rex Damory?"

"I will not."

"Do you still choose suffering?"

"I choose it."

Would death never come? Had he been there for years? Eventually unconsciousness came to his aid.

When his brain cleared again, he heard voices.

"Perchance if he saw him," said Nicholas Leslie.

"Someone might see me," objected the Duke. "I am very ill at Warwick, remember."

"It is not five yet and all are asleep, Your Grace. Besides a mere handful are here." He turned, released Rex, and dragged him to his feet.

"Edward himself shall release you," said the Duke.

"He cannot, for I have sworn, my lord."

"Come," was the curt reply.

Rex followed, though every step was agony. They entered the King's apartments and, at Richard's gesture, Rex went on to the sleeping chamber. The boys were resting quietly, and Rex bent over the King.

He lay there untouched by care or sorrow, a smile upon his lips, as if his dreams were pleasant ones.

"Edward," Rex whispered softly.

There was ominous silence, and he touched Edward's hand. It was cold in death.

"O Edward, Edward!" he cried and he who had suffered so gallantly a few moments before, knelt sobbing like a child at his friend's side.

"Does not the King release you?" asked Richard's cold voice. "Will you take allegiance to me now?"

Rex sprang to his feet, pain, fear, everything forgotten in his indignation. "Traitor, villain, murderer, do you think I would ever swear fealty to *you*?"

"Remember," Richard warned him.

"I care not. Punish me as you will. I defy your worst." He knelt again by Edward's side and took the cold hand in his. "Edward of England, in life and in death, I am your liegeman and loyal servant," he said clearly. Then, rising, he faced Richard. "I have taken my allegiance, Your Grace."

A blow from a gauntleted hand, a vision of the Duke's angry face, and Rex fell senseless at Richard's feet.

VIII

Leslie Tower

WHAT HAPPENED after that fall in the King's room, Rex never clearly knew. There were long nights of pain and endless days of delirium with a vague consciousness of a journey in a horse litter under the care of rough guardsmen. But at last there came a time when the fever left him, and he opened his eyes on strange quarters. It was a room high in a tower. From an open though barred window, a salty breeze from the sea swept in. The high carved bed on which he lay was luxurious; the paneled walls were of solid oak, while on the table lay a maiden's work of rich embroidery.

The door opened to admit Ruth. Rex started at her in bewilderment.

"You here? Where am I?"

"So you have recovered your senses at last." She walked over to him. "You must not talk, Rex Damory, so says Nurse Gillian."

"I thought I was in the Tower—I saw the King dead—Just tell me this, Ruth, was it a dream?"

130

"You are not to talk," she repeated. "How can I tell what your delirium was. You have raved enough to make one believe any wild tale. I bid you sleep."

Rex said no more. He knew too well that it was no dream, and with closed eyes he lay there facing his pain and loneliness. Ruth went back to the table and took up her work.

"He is sleeping, I think," he heard her say a little later as the door was open again.

"And you must go out, Mistress Ruth. I will keep watch and ward," said a woman's voice, and Rex saw that the woman she had called Nurse Gillian had come. She was an old woman with kindly eyes and a wrinkled face and, to his amazement, he saw Ruth bend and kiss her with a real love light in her eyes. Once the door had closed, the old woman came over to him and bent over the bed.

"You are better, laddie," she said. "What ails you? You are greeting, not sleeping now."

"It is the King. I did not dream it all," Rex faltered. "He is dead and I am all alone."

"Aye, they say he died of fever some three weeks agone. But he loved you, did he not? And love goes on."

"Love goes on," Rex repeated, and the old wrinkled hand came over his.

"God comfort you," Nurse Gillian whispered. "Puir laddie. You are Lady Elsie's bairn, are you not?"

"Did you know my mother?"

"Have you never heard of Gillian, her auld Scotch nurse? But you were a wee one when she died. Aye, I nursed her and dressed her for her bridal, puir mitherless lassie that she was. She was bright as a sunbeam that day, and bright as a sunbeam she was to the last, I have na doot. You are talking too much, laddie. Rest you now."

"Just one more thing. How did I come here, Nurse Gillian?"

"Sir Nicholas brought you himself wi' three loons o' men-at-arms to tend a lad at death's door. To the right about I sent them, Sir Nicholas and all. He told me and Mistress Ruth to tend you and that he would come again."

"And this is my mother's home?"

"Nay, this is the tower of Leslie. Hers was Deventry. Sir Nicholas owns this place now, and he sent me here to bide wi' Mistress Ruth."

Rex lay silent and soon fell asleep. It was the turning point of his illness, and slowly his strength returned, and though there were long hours of weakness, the fever did not come back.

He grew to love Nurse Gillian, and through the weary hours of convalescence, she told him the stories of the mother who, up to this time, had been but a vague memory. With Ruth, he was usually silent, for her tongue was no gentler than of old. It was not until the first day that he was allowed to get up that he questioned her as he lay resting after the venture of his pilgrimage about the room.

"Am I a prisoner?" he asked.

"If I said aye, you would whine about it like the veriest maid."

"If you said nay, the surprise would almost bring the fever back."

"Then why ask foolish questions?"

"Because these would trouble Nurse Gillian. I know I am a prisoner, but how much freedom have I got?"

"The battlements and the grounds, if you will give your word to speak to no one and make no effort to escape. Sir Nicholas said that you would be loon enough to keep such a promise."

"I am glad that he has found out that much truth about Damorys at last. Well, I give my word. When does he come?"

"When you are strong again. He said you must have fully recovered."

"I see. He will have to wait a little."

"You will not attempt to escape?" she asked.

"I see no opportunity in any case and even if there were and I gave back my parole, I could not leave you to bear the brunt of Sir Nicholas Leslie's wrath. Methinks, he has his vengeance close at hand and he will have to take it."

"And you are not afraid?"

"I faced the worst in the Tower, the night the King died."

"And you think that there was foul play?"

"I know it. I saw him and little Duke Richard as they lay dead, and both had been alive and fairly well a few hours before."

"You are wondrous clever. Well, since you have given your word, you have the freedom of the place."

Rex said no more, but as he lay there, Ruth stole many a look at his quiet face. He had endured suffering. He was facing death now. She shivered again. "I could not do it," she said to herself.

Months came and went, and little by little health and strength came back to Rex. Nicholas Leslie was detained at court, for conspiracy was rife, and there was no leisure for thoughts of private vengeance. Rumors of discontent came in to Leslie Tower through strolling packmen and wandering minstrels. The storm muttered more ominously in their own neighborhood, for Nicholas Leslie had never been aught but a stern lord, and the Torsmen were in a state of smouldering wrath. Ruth declared the glowering faces and muttered words meant nothing, but Rex, as they rode or walked together, began to wonder if a real outbreak was not at hand. The winter passed, and the spring came, later than in Dorset, but the hills were bright with gorse, the combs thick with cowslip and primrose. Then came summer with all its beauty, and still Nicholas tarried in London.

Rex and Ruth found themselves by very isolation setting up an unspoken comradeship. True, her tongue was as shrewish as of old, and more than once Rex's hot temper blazed out under her taunts, but he found himself watching for her coming, and rides and walks were dull to Ruth when Rex tarried at home. She would not have owned it to him, but her face grew white as she saw approaching horsemen, and she feared the coming of Nicholas far more than Rex did himself.

The autumn did not bring him, and Christmas came and went quietly enough, but on a cold day in January, as Rex came up the park, he found Ruth waiting for him on the terrace.

"Sir Nicholas has come, Rex."

His face whitened a little. "And he wants me?"

"Later. He is supping now and will seek you in the tower. I was to bid you go there."

"I will go." She hesitated a moment, then she held out her hand. "I am sorry that I called you a coward, Rex. I am sorry for your peril now."

He smiled as he took her hand in his. "You have done much for me, Ruth. I thank you for this and for these months of companionship," he said.

He went straight up the stairs. Nicholas would make him wait, he knew. Anything that could add to the nervous tension he was obliged to endure would be used. He walked over to the window, resisting an impulse to pace restlessly up and down.

"God keep me strong," he prayed.

The sun had set, and it was fully an hour later before the familiar step sounded on the stair and the door was pushed open to admit Sir Nicholas. The man attending him bore a torch which he placed in a sconce on the wall before he withdrew. Nicholas seated himself at the table.

"Well, Rex Damory?"

"I greet you, Sir Nicholas. What do you want of me?"

"I see that you have recovered."

"Fully, thanks to the good care that I have received."

"Our gracious lord, King Richard, is merciful and you have had time to think. Will you sign that paper now?"

"Methought that I had made that plain enough at our last interview, Sir Nicholas. I have not changed my mind."

"You refuse?"

"Emphatically."

Sir Nicholas clenched his hands in baffled rage. Rex had changed. This was no frightened or excited lad who faced him now, but one wholly beyond his reach. He studied the quiet eyes in silence.

"You will throw your life away for a mere whim?" he asked at last.

"Not for a whim, Sir Nicholas, but for love of my comrade and my King."

"Who is dead. How can it harm him if you sign now?"

"Love and friendship live on, Sir Nicholas. Dog were I indeed to blacken his memory."

"You are a visionary still. Well, do you yield your life?"

"I am in your hands, Sir Nicholas. Do I die tonight or must I suffer in the Tower?"

Nicholas Leslie smiled coldly. "You do not understand your choice, Rex Damory. We plan no spectacular ending for you. Nor are we minded that the Red Rose shall honor you as a hero and martyr. I have a debt to pay not only to you, but also to Hugh Damory."

Rex made a little gesture of surrender. "Well, pay it."

"You defy me? Well then, listen and mark my words. You say that you will not blacken Edward's memory. Your own will be too dark for even merciful forgetfulness. The political side of the affair will be dropped. You will end your life as a condemned murderer."

Rex laughed. "Are you planning to be the victim, Sir Nicholas?"

"We need no other. Have you forgotten the verderer of Epping Forest? Ah, that touches you at last, drives the color from your face!"

But if Nicholas looked for an outcry, he was disappointed. Rex kept strict hold on himself. "You will find it hard to get 'twelve good men and true' to convict me on that account, Sir Nicholas Leslie. Try it, if you choose."

"The compassing of the charge will require a little time, but it will be unescapable, my young springald. Nor need you plan to bring wild charges against the King. They will not be heeded. This is your choice, either you sign the paper that we need or you endure this shameful end. Which will you choose?"

"The keeping of my honor clear. The shameful end affects others, not myself. My father, in the light of the heavenly country, knows the truth, those whom I love will not judge me guilty whatever your false witnesses and packed jury may decree. Moreover, God can show the right."

"When the noose comes about your neck, we shall hear another tale." Nicholas rose. "I shall ride for London in the morn. You may look for me in two weeks' time with the warrant for your arrest. Remember, Ruth is hostage for your safety. If you run away, we shall bring her to trial as accessory."

"You need not fear, Sir Nicholas. Rex Damory has not yet come to the pass of sheltering behind maids."

"I will leave you then. If you change your mind, perchance the King will permit the signing. Otherwise, you will not see another Candlemas."

Rex bowed in silence, and with angry eyes Nicholas took his departure. Once again, he had failed.

"You are an obstinate lad," he flung back over his shoulder. "Have your own way."

Rex watched him down the stairs and then walked over to the window where the moors lay a mass of purple in the moonlight with the sea beyond. There was no tumult in Rex's heart this time. His foes were relentless, and he had no intention of yielding to them. "I will face it all when it comes," he said resolutely to himself. "God will give me the strength that I need."

Early in the morning he saw Sir Nicholas start forth with Tyrrell and Forrest, and Rex noted that the sullen Torsmen gave him no ovation and stood scowling, as their lord departed. Rex went downstairs. There was no use in worrying Ruth or Nurse Gillian. He would keep things to himself. Ruth caught her breath with a little sigh of relief when she saw him.

"Is all well, Rex?" she asked.

"For the present, Ruth," he answered.

He caught a new light in her face, but she covered up her satisfaction quickly. "We cannot ride today, Rex. Sir Nicholas says that the Torsmen be affected with Red Rose treachery, and that we must bide at home."

"What is the matter with them, Ruth?"

"Sir Nicholas arrested three of them for poaching yesterday. They have been angry ever since he forced the young men to enlist and go with him to London. No one has ever been able to manage the Torsmen, Rex."

"They do not look manageable. Do you want to go to the shore, Ruth? We might take the boat, if a ride is out of the question."

She nodded and seized her cloak at once. During the day, she was very quiet, and Rex caught a wistfulness in her face more than once. It was at midnight that her voice roused him from a sound sleep.

"Rex, Rex, please wake. I want you; I want you! I am so frightened! What shall we do?"

He sprang up and, flinging on his clothes, was beside her in a few minutes. Outside, pandemonium raged. Flashing torches and angry voices added to the terror of the scene. Ruth slipped a cold hand into his.

"It is the Torsmen. They have revolted. Hear how they batter at the door."

"Get you out, my bairnies." Nurse Gillian came to them. "The postern is safe, Mistress Ruth."

"But you, Nurse Gillian?"

"I am in no danger, lassie. I will mingle with them; there be women in the crowd. It is you that they are seeking and they will not heed me. Get her out and over the down eastward, Lord Rex. These folk be ill to cross."

"Burn the tower; burn the tower!" came the shout. "Death to them all; smoke them out."

"Get a heavy dark cloak, Ruth," Rex commanded. "We will make for the stables."

The girl obeyed him. In a moment they were outside the postern. The old nurse slipped out to the front but was back very quickly.

"This is your chance," she whispered. "The Torsmen have fired the tower and the smoke is rising fast!"

"We must have horses," Rex said. "You must come too, Nurse Gillian. We will not leave you."

"Whist ye, laddie, I should only hamper ye."

"That matters not. Now I will get the horses. Bide here in the shadow of the trees and come to the stable when I give the owl hoot."

They watched him go. He was soon in the stable loosening the frightened horses. Four he turned loose and saddled the remaining three.

"Hoo, hoo," he called.

Slipping from tree to tree, they joined him. He placed Nurse Gillian on one horse, swung Ruth's light form to a second one, and mounted the third himself. They rode cautiously through the park, but once on the moor, they went at full speed. The flames from the tower shot up, and their foes saw them. A howl went up. But Rex's plan of leaving the rebels horseless delayed them, and though two flying arrows came perilously near, the fugitives were soon out of range and reasonably free from pursuit.

Ruth suddenly caught Rex's arm and pointed to a flare in the west. "They are burning Deventry," she cried.

"Then we will make for Dorset Downs," Rex said cheerily as he turned in a wide sweep from the fires which marked their foes. It was not until, in the dawning, and they came to a half ruined cottage, that he drew rein.

"We will rest here for an hour and breathe the horses," he said. He lifted Ruth down and helped Nurse Gillian who heaved a sigh of relief.

"I'm ower auld for sich wark as this," she said.

In the hut, they found a rude stone pallet which Rex made fairly comfortable by piling their cloaks upon it. Nurse Gillian lay there, and Ruth sat on the floor beside her. Rex looked at them.

"I will look to the horses and keep watch. Try to rest a little, Ruth," he urged.

He stood outside. The glare was slowly dying down. The moors were very still, and the wind sounded eerily in the trees. Suddenly a light step sounded beside him, and Ruth slipped her hand into his. She raised a white, tear-stained face.

"Is aught wrong with Nurse Gillian?" he asked anxiously.

"Nay, she is sleeping, but I could not stay there alone. I am afraid, Rex: I have never been afraid before."

"Poor little maid, you are tired out and cold too. But I dare not kindle a fire." He drew her under the eaves of the house, sat down and put his arm about her. She drew close.

"It is all so horrible, Rex. What shall we do and where shall we go?"

"Morning will decide that. Dawn is breaking now. Do not be afraid. God is watching us still." He smiled down at her, and again her cold fingers touched his.

"I have been so hateful to you, Rex."

"You are no Red Rose rebel, little sister."

"It does not seem to matter tonight. You could have joined the Torsmen and have been safe, and yet you have risked flying arrows and their vengeance, if they capture us, all for a maid who hated you."

"Nay, for my sister, Ruth."

"I have come to know what you are tonight, though I have wanted to tell you that I was sorry before. Will you forgive me?"

"With all my heart, little sister."

"I am not your *little* sister. We be twins."

"I feel the older, Ruth. There has been so much to think of and to fight for, and I have been so alone."

"You will not be alone any longer, for I stand beside you, Rex."

He bent and kissed her, rejoicing that he had kept his peril from her. Silently, they watched the dawn.

Suddenly, Ruth started and bent forward listening. "There be horses coming, Rex."

He pulled her to her feet. "Get Nurse Gillian, Ruth. I will loosen our steeds." He worked quickly, but as he brought the horses to the door and Ruth with the old nurse joined him, he saw the approaching riders were two in number, a maid and an elder woman.

"Why, it is Joyce and Lady Margaret!" Ruth cried.

"Ruth Leslie!" Joyce galloped up and drew rein. "Did they burn you out too? Deventry is gone and we are homeless."

"Methinks that Leslie Tower is a ruin too," said Ruth. "I know not if they attacked the Manor House in Leslie Village. Here is Rex, Joyce."

Joyce held out both hands and, at the light in her eyes, Ruth's old jealousy flamed up. Rex turned to her.

"We had best seek refuge all together, little sister," he suggested.

Ruth's sudden anger died. She drew the older woman forward. "Lady Margaret, this is my brother, Rex Damory," she said, and the newcomer held out her hand.

"Elsie's lad?" she questioned. "I have often heard of you, boy. I loved your mother well."

Rex greeted her warmly. He could see that the stress of the night had told on her as on Nurse Gillian.

"How did you get to Devon, Joyce?" he asked. "I thought that you were with Princess Elizabeth."

"First Ruth and then I received orders to go," Joyce answered. "Poor little Princess, my heart aches for her, but I hope she is with her mother still. Sir Nicholas bade me go to Deventry and sent Lady Margaret, who has been fairy godmother and kinswoman to Ruth and me, to keep me company. We were warned last night that the Torsmen were out, and we got away just before the place was fired. Sir Nicholas has stirred up a pretty hornet's nest."

"What shall we do next?" Ruth asked.

"We must press on," Rex answered. "We are too near the seat of the trouble at present. Perhaps we can shelter at some farmhouse, till we make plans."

"Why not go to Damory?" Joyce suggested. "Among your own folk, we are sure to find friends. For food, there is a farmhouse not far away where I know the tenants. You bide here with Nurse Gillian and Lady Margaret, Rex, and Ruth and I will get provisions for us all."

"Do you think that would be safe?" Rex asked reluctantly.

"Quite. Come, Ruth. The others must rest."

Rex lifted Ruth to the saddle. The two girls were soon out of sight. But before they reached the farmhouse, Joyce drew rein.

"I want to ask a plain question, Ruth," she said. "Are you friend or foe to Rex?"

"Do you need to ask that now? I have found out what my brother is."

"Then you are willing to help him, Ruth? He is in sore danger."

"I hoped that it had passed."

"Sir Nicholas came to Deventry on his way from Leslie Tower. He would tell me little, but he said he had the upper hand of Rex Damory now, and that his vengeance would be complete in a few weeks."

"He told me there would be no state trial," Ruth said. "But he laughed and announced that Rex would rue his obstinacy yet."

"Then he is planning something horrible, Ruth. That is why I proposed this refuge. Rex will never run away, but I thought among his own people he might be protected. We shall gain time here, for not only are the Torsmen out but the Duke of Buckingham is in the field and Henry of Richmond may land at any moment. Now I will ride on and get the food. We do not want anyone to track us through the farmhouse. If Sir Nicholas thinks that you and Rex perished in the fire at Leslie Tower so much the better."

Ruth agreed, and a few moments later Joyce was back with the supplies. The farmer had warned her to push on quickly, for the trouble was spreading. The two girls rode back, and, after a brief repast, the whole party started for Dorset border. They crossed it soon after noonday, and it was not long after dusk when they came in sight of Damory. The west wing was intact, with Sir Hugo's tower and the chapel. The rest was a blackened ruin.

"Shall we shelter here tonight or seek Blandford?" Rex asked.

Ruth's quick eyes caught the signs of habitation. "There is someone living here, Rex. Let us try here first."

Rex rode on. He knocked, and an old man came to the door. There was a cry of joy, a shout, and out poured a number of men and women who fell to kissing his hands in eager greeting.

"Rance, Roger! How came you all here?" Rex cried joyously.

"We have sheltered here in safety for some months, young

lord," said Rance. "We have been mourning you as dead."

"Will you make ready then for me and for our guests?" Rex said. "I see you know Lady Margaret Deventry and Nurse Gillian too. The maids you have seen before, Mistress Joyce Deventry and my sister, Mistress Ruth."

The squire's face hardened at the last name, but the girl held out her hand to him. "I marvel not that you have no welcome for me," she told him. "But I am a Damory, Rance, and I am fighting with you for your young lord now."

"God keep you, Mistress Ruth," was all Rance said, but Ruth knew that she had won a friend.

SO THE life at Damory began, a quiet one enough with the sole drawback that Rex would not seek safety in France. The fugitives kept closely to the court, and Rance took care that no strangers were admitted, for he would not allow provisions to be purchased save at a distance, lest the amount might cause comment. But Nicholas Leslie made no move. Roger brought back the tidings that Devonshire was in rebellion and that an army had been sent there. Then came the news that Nicholas was on an embassy to France, for Richard was making an effort to secure the person of Henry of Richmond from Brittany. The embassy was delayed, and no sooner had it returned than the Duke of Buckingham's rebellion brought all White Rose men to Richard's standard. The winter months passed, and the summer of 1485 found all but Rance and the two maids sure that all would be well.

"We could not all go," Rex insisted. "My best chance is to bide here at home. Later, when things are quieter, we will try to escape."

"Rex is as obstinate as one of our moor ponies, Rance," Ruth complained one hot day in July. "This idea that I shall suffer if he goes is ridiculous. Can you do nothing at all?"

"Damory's men will not let Damory's lord suffer, Mistress Ruth," Rance said sturdily. "What now?" as Simon came up to them.

"A messenger is seeking you, Rance the squire," he said. "My lord of Richmond has landed and calls for Damory's men."

"We are saved then, Mistress Ruth," Rance said joyfully. "Even my obstinate young lord will not refuse this call. He will take the field with Damory and leave a strong guard here."

IX

Bosworth Field

R EX, YOU will go?" Ruth pleaded.

"I know not if you will be safe, Ruth. Were I sure of that, my duty would be clear. The Red Rose has called."

"You might give me credit for a little sense myself," Ruth protested. "Leave Roger here with me. Sir Nicholas knows not where we are and probably thinks that I died at Leslie Tower. If, by ill hap, my lord of Richmond is defeated, I promise you that I will not wait but go at once to France."

"On your word, you will promise this?"

"On my solemn word of honor. Does that satisfy you?"

"Fully, Ruth. Then will I go, please God, to return soon and make a real home here for you. Now I will seek Rance and Joyce."

"She is borrowing trouble, Rex. She has made up her mind that Sir Nicholas will get his hands upon you. Go and comfort her."

Rex smiled as he sought the garden. Joyce was there, gathering clustering roses, her face troubled and worn. She turned at his footstep.

"I am going, Joyce. Ruth has promised, if aught should go amiss, that she will not wait but will go at once to France. I want you to go with her in that case, Joyce. Why are you crying?"

"I fear so for you, Rex," she sobbed. "You will be captured and killed by Sir Nicholas and that evil King."

Rex laughed. "You are borrowing a goodly load of trouble, Joyce. I do not mean to give that kinsman of mine any such chance. The future is brighter than for many a long day. It seems as if the Red Rose might be coming to her own, and if, as is rumored, a marriage between our Princess and the Earl of Richmond takes place, this war, which has wrought such woe for England through three generations, will be at an end. There will be union between the Roses and peace for us all."

She shivered as she looked at his scarred hands. "I am afraid, Rex."

"Would you really have me play the coward, Joyce? Were I your brother, what would you bid me do? It is plain duty to go to my Prince's side, and have I the right to hold back? God has brought me through many dangers, can He not protect me in this one?"

Her eyes grew steadfast. "You are right, and I am wrong, Rex. Come and let me help you to make ready. I suppose that you will start soon."

"Within two hours." He stooped and picked up her flowers. "Give me one, Joyce."

She held out a crimson bud. "Here is the badge of your dear Cause," she said; "take this one too, of white, for Edward's sake and Ruth's."

Rex took them and the two went into the house. Two hours later, with Ruth's snood on his helm and the two roses resting on his breast, he rode away in the midst of his men, old Rance

close beside him with his wrinkled face aglow with pride. Two
days later, he rode into Henry of Richmond's camp where men
of both sides, weary of Richard and his misrule, were pouring
in, and the next day the march began.

Three days later, the armies met at Bosworth Field. It was
almost nightfall, and after an attempt on both sides to seize the
low hills at the left, an attempt which ended in the vantage of
Sir William Stanley of Richard's force, the two armies encamped
at opposite sides of the plain. Each general knew that the conflict of the next day would be decisive and contented himself
with posting guards about his camp and waiting for daylight.
The armies, with the exception of Sir William Stanley's eight
hundred men, were evenly matched, for all along the march
Richmond's force had been augmented by Red and White alike.
Many of the most powerful White Rose lords came in that
night. They had doubted the tales of murder and wrong at first,
but had found them all too true, generally at their own cost.

There was no sleep for either side. Richmond and his men
spent the night in prayer and vigil, for each man knew that he
could expect no mercy should Richard be victorious. From the
Yorkist camp came the sound of music and merriment, for there
too was confidence in the fact that Richard of Gloucester had
never lost a fight. Those off duty gathered in tents and around
campfires and jested and sang and feasted, for their lord had
given orders that food was not to be spared. But Richard himself
did not join in the merrymaking. He sat alone in his own tent,
hung with rich draperies, poring over a map and making plan
after plan of the coming battle. The midnight hour struck, but
still he worked on feverishly. The crown he had won had not
brought him happiness. His eyes were tired, and the deep drawn
lines and shadows in his face told of sleepless nights. Hag-ridden
did he find himself to be. Not once in the two chequered years
of his power had he felt safe. Dread of the assassin, fear of rebel-

lion, and constant quarrels haunted his waking hours. Buckingham, his friend, had revolted and now lay in his traitor's grave. Two months ago, Edward, his only son, had died suddenly of fever, and the loss had shaken and broken him. He thought often of that scene in his youth when he had stood facing Margaret, the Red Rose Queen, with the dead body of her young son Edward between them and his blood on Richard's dagger and hand. On Edward of York's line had her punishment been laid, and here in his own house, in the person of the only one he had ever loved, it had again been fulfilled. Now the Red Rose, long supposed vanquished, had risen again.

He rose and paced restlessly up and down. The revelry of his camp formed a strange contrast to the sound of prayer and psalm which came from his rival's side of the field. Something very like fear was lurking in Richard's eyes. Edward's pleading voice seemed to ring in his ears; Anne, his dead wife, haunted his thoughts, while, through the gloom of this hour before the dawn, his brothers seemed to watch him with reproachful eyes and he heard again Elizabeth Woodville's solemn words. The sighing of the night wind and the hooting of the owls made him start and throw himself shuddering on his sleepless couch.

"My liege." Nicholas Leslie entered the tent unceremoniously. "I have evil tidings. Richmond's army is nearly as large as our own. Save for Sir William Stanley's force, we are evenly matched."

"And he?"

"Is camped on the hills between us. I do not trust him, my lord. I told you that weeks agone."

"And I secured him. If he plays us false, his son dies and he knows it. I told him that George's life was the price of his fealty. Have you sent him any message?"

"I bade him join us, but he sent back word that any move on his part would mean that Richmond would occupy the hills before we could replace his man. The worst of it is that he is right."

"It was not like your caution to allow him to get there in the first place, Nicholas. But any move we make now would mean an instant attack. We shall have to leave him alone. Anything else?"

"Rex Damory is with Richmond."

"Rex Damory! Methought he perished in the fire at Leslie Tower?"

"So I thought, Sire. I could find no trace of him nor of Ruth. But Joyce Deventry also disappeared, and the servants said that she left Deventry an hour before the attack. She may have warned them. Be that as it may, he has appeared and with what he knows may bring half of England about our ears. His very coming is ominous. He has ever balked us. The fates and the stars in their courses fight for Rex Damory."

Richard smiled evilly. "I look at the matter otherwise, my friend. We are in the ascendant. Tomorrow night, the Red Rose will lie crushed and broken. Richmond and Rex Damory will be in our power. We will have our revenge, and a sweet one it will be, Nicholas."

I tell you that you shall not have Rex. I am the King; I will protect him.

White and shaken, Richard sprang to his feet. Had he really heard the words?

"My liege, my liege, are you ill?" Nicholas cried.

Richard shrank back shivering. "It is nothing. I thought I heard—but it is nothing. Tomorrow, we will work our will on Rex Damory—"

I tell you that you shall not have Rex. I am the King; I will protect him.

Was it really Edward's white face that he saw? Was it his murdered nephew's voice which rang in his ears? Were Edward's eyes looking into his with stern denunciation in them? Was the nightmare of his nights translated into day? A cry of agony broke from the guilty King.

"What is it?" Nicholas cried.

"Look, there he stands! Edward, Edward, avaunt! I bid you go. You shall not torment me. I defy you. Ah-h, Rivers, Woodville, Grey, Hastings, my brothers! Nicholas, Nicholas, bid them go!" He sank shuddering on the ground. "Ah-h, touch me not. Kill me then. Brother, Brother, ask not for your sons. I did not slay them, not with mine own hand. Look not at me. Am I going mad?"

All through the rest of the night, he lay there pleading with the specters his fancy conjured up, while Nicholas, in terror himself, strove to soothe him, till as the sun burst over Bosworth Field the ringing trumpets of Richmond sounded the mustering call. Richard rose and girded himself for the struggle with trembling hands. As he left the tent with Nicholas, he looked back and spoke as to someone standing there. "You have your wish, Edward. Would that I had died a boy at Castle York."

Outside, the Duke of Norfolk was waiting. "I fear treachery, my liege," he said, drawing the King aside. "I found this pinned to my tent this morning."

Richard took the scroll. *Fockery of Norfolk, be not so bold*, he read. *For Diccon, your master, is bought and sold.*

"But what does it mean?" asked Nicholas Leslie.

"Stanley," Richard returned fiercely. "Were I perfectly sure, I would behead young George this instant. Yet it were madness to risk it. But see that he is guarded well, Nicholas, no matter what need of men be ours. We will avenge ourselves on Sir William for this anxiety later. Now to the battle. Richard is himself again, and we will face the issue."

In brave array the two armies confronted one another while the early sunbeams glittered on Sir William Stanley's serried ranks of spears camped between. A herald rode forward at Richard's command.

"Richard by the grace of God, King of England and of France and Lord of Ireland, proclaims free pardon to all in arms against him who, forsaking their present rebellion, now join his standard, save only Henry, Earl of Richmond, John, Earl of Fortescue, and Reginald, Lord of Damory. On the head of each of these, alive or dead, is placed a price of one thousand marks."

Not one of Richmond's force stirred. The Earl turned to John Fortescue.

"Where is our fellow?" Raising his visor, Henry of Richmond held out his hand. "Greeting, my fellow criminal. What have you, a lad in years, done to be ranked with a deep-dyed traitor like myself?"

"I can count those crimes my honor now," Rex answered. "I incurred the hate of my lord of Gloucester when I was in attendance upon his nephew, King Edward the Fifth. Nigh on two years ago, I came near to sharing his fate, and though I have escaped to now, Duke Richard does not forget."

"You are the Red Rose rebel of whom I have heard much," Henry answered. "I have heard of your deeds, my lord, and likewise I have not forgotten that your brave father laid down his life for my sake. Fight beside me, Rex Damory. It is victory or death for us at least. To the onslaught, gentlemen. St. George for Merry England!"

Henry flung down his gage as he spoke, and the conflict began, a fierce and hard-fought field, for the armies were evenly matched and swayed to and fro in indecisive conflict while Sir William Stanley remained inactive upon the hills. Well was it for Henry of Richmond that Rex fought beside him that day, for twice in the desperate conflict his weapon turned the blow aimed at the Earl's life.

"Well done, Rex Damory; if we come out of this, I shall not forget," Henry promised, as the foe rushed on.

Rex smiled and fought on with desperate determination. The

fight surged hottest about them, for all Richard's efforts were directed at disabling or slaying his rival. But still the battle hung in the balance, and the sides swayed to and fro. Now the right wing of Richmond would gain a slight advantage, now the left wing of Gloucester swept slightly forward, but always one counterbalanced the other. Only one person was inactive. Clad in full panoply, Sir William Stanley watched from his height with the close line of spears behind him, while his officers and attendants reined in fretting and champing steeds with steady hands.

"Why does he not charge?" Richard cried to Nicholas Leslie. "By my troth, but he shall pay for this. A single charge from him and the battle is won."

"He says he is waiting for the best moment," Nicholas called back. "His force is moving now. I thought he would hardly dare to disregard that last summons."

"Rally our men for the center, Norfolk," Richard commanded. "Hold them till the onslaught sounds."

A single bugle note rang on the air. Richard looked eagerly at the advancing host, when with a cry of "England and the Red Rose," Sir William Stanley charged right into the ranks of York.

It was too late now to think of vengeance. Bewildered by a double foe, Richard's men bore back. The White Rose was fighting for its life and, gritting his teeth in helpless rage, Richard knew that the battle was lost.

"By the light of bright Saint George's crown, Richmond shall not survive the day," he shouted, as by exercise of sheer strength he and his personal bodyguard fought their way to the banner under which Henry stood. Down went the standard bearer under the furious charge; down went Sir John Cheney, dead in his master's service, and with him the two esquires, leaving Richmond fighting hand to hand with Gloucester. It was an unequal contest, for Richard was the most skillful knight of his time, and outmatched his opponent in every way. But Henry was no shirker and stood his ground with the courage worthy of his great line.

"Down with you, Richmond!" Richard lunged at the Earl.

"Down with you, false Gloucester!" Rex's weapon came between, and his shield with the glittering cross of Damory turned the blow. With a cry of triumph, Nicholas Leslie spurred forward.

"Face to face at last, Rex Damory," he shouted. "On guard!" He had totally forgotten Richard and his peril in his hate. He rushed at Rex, and another unequal conflict began. Rex was obliged to turn his attention to this new foe. Nicholas was desperate and fought recklessly and, on that wild day, Rex was distracted by Richmond's danger.

"'Ware, my lord, 'ware!" he cried, as he saw Richard lunge again while Norfolk attacked from the rear. Then he went down under Nicholas Leslie's half parried blow, just as Sir William Stanley fought his way to Henry's side. The fight went on above him, till Richard fell, covered with wounds, and Nicholas turned and fled. The sounds of conflict died down and the Red Rose trumpets blew the recall. Sir William Stanley lifted the battered circlet which had fallen from Richard's helm and placed it on the victor.

"Long live King Henry the Seventh," he cried, and the shout was taken up and echoed over the field.

"Thanks, brave friends," Richmond said as he received the homage of his lords. Then he bent over Rex and touched him with his sword.

"Thrice have you saved my life this day. Rise up, Sir Reginald Damory," he said.

The moon shone down on Bosworth Field some hours later as Rex stood there looking at the scene, the heaps of slain, still forms and battered armor. The cries of the wounded had ceased, for Henry, merciful in his victory, had cared for friend and foe alike. Rex was restless with the pain of his wounds, and old memories were troubling him. Lord of rich acres and knighted on the field of battle, the old longing for his friend was upon him. He found himself longing anew for the sound of Edward's voice and the touch of Edward's hand.

The Wars of the Roses were done. The conflict which had drenched England in blood was ended. Henry of Lancaster, gallant York, brave Warwick, and young Prince Edward had fallen. Rivers, Grey and Hastings, the boy King and his brother had been murdered, and now the last of York's ill-fated line lay dead on Bosworth Field. Rex thought of the evil, storm-tossed face he had glimpsed as he himself fell. The two brief years of kingship had not brought happiness to Richard Gloucester.

Rex turned to happier thoughts. Out of the carnage, a new England was rising, an England in which Rex himself might play a part. His face grew eager as he thought of it, a vision within the realm of possibility, an England which would be a land of progress, of learning and venturing. With eagerness, Rex turned to the thoughts of it as he made his way back towards his tent. His unwounded hand sought his breast and drew out the faded roses. He smiled as he looked at them. How Ruth and Joyce would delight in his honors and his safety! He could make a home at Damory now. What would become of Joyce? Whither had her father fled, and how was she to be secured from his influence? Poor Joyce, her problem was a hard one. If Lady Margaret would stay, there might be a home for her in Damory. Aye, perhaps some day, he might bring Joyce home in very truth. He lifted the Red Rose to his lips.

"Do you love the badge of your dear Cause so much that you treasure it thus, Rex Damory?" asked Henry's teasing voice. "Will you come to my court to heal your wounds, or must I send you back to your Dorset Downs?"

"My sister Ruth is at Damory, Your Grace."

"Did she bestow roses? Nay, flush not, lad, there is no shame in treasuring a maiden's gift."

"Nor need I hide it, Your Grace. Mistress Joyce gave me these flowers, and I have dreams of a future yet to be fulfilled."

"God grant it may, lad. Joyce Deventry? She is Nicholas Leslie's maid, is she not?"

"Aye, her loneliness is great. Deventry was burned, and she has neither home nor friends."

"We will befriend her. For the next few days there is much to do. With Richard dead and Lady Elizabeth my affianced, there is not like to be much fighting. I must push on to London and Castle York. Your wound will prevent hard riding for a few days, and so you had best stay with the rear guard. Send word to your maids to assure them of your safety and honors and bid them be in readiness to come to court."

X

Bitter Woe

I BRING good news, Rex Damory," the King said some days later when he returned to his camp. "London has tendered her submission and practically all the other large towns have followed her example. You had best make your way back to Damory, heal your wounds and bring your maids to London for the coronation. I go to woo my little Princess, and, God willing, she will have a welcome and a place for both Joyce and Ruth."

"I thank Your Grace and will make ready," Rex answered.

His thoughts were pleasant ones as he made his way back to his tent, pitched under the lee of a hill. The trials of the past years were over. Life lay clear before him at last. For Ruth, there would be her share of Damory's broad lands, for Joyce, a place at court with perchance a brighter future at hand. Some day another Leslie bride might come to Damory. *And maiden's hand bring harmony and joy and peace to Damory*, Rex murmured to himself. Not one misgiving crossed his mind concerning the last clause of Damory's punishment. He lifted the tent flap and entered, then stood in some surprise, for there rose from the seat beside the table a tall man in battered armor, muffled in a travel-worn cloak.

"What do you want?" Rex asked. "How came you here?"

"It is like your carelessness to leave the place unguarded," sneered the other. "I want you, Rex Damory."

"*Nicholas Leslie!*"

"Aye, Nicholas Leslie. You thought you had outwitted me, Rex Damory, but you will find out your mistake."

"You are daring, Nicholas Leslie," Rex said sternly. "There is a price on your head, and yet you have ventured into our camp."

"Quite safely." Nicholas shrugged his shoulder. "Arrest me if you will. Slay me if you choose. The brunt falls not on me but on the maids."

"Ruth and Joyce?"

"Ruth and Joyce. They are in my power and if I fail to come home—well, my men have orders."

"What proof do you bring?"

"My word."

"Which is worth nothing," said Rex curtly.

"A messenger from Damory preceded me. Here comes Rance. Hear what he says."

"Stand back in the shadow then," Rex ordered, as Rance came in.

"There are ill tidings, my lord," the squire said sorrowfully. "Roger has just ridden posthaste from Damory. The maids are lost."

"When?"

"Two days after the battle. They rode forth as usual with Roger for a morning ride. A lad came up and spoke to Mistress Ruth, and after conversing with him, she rode back to Mistress Joyce. They bade Roger return and send word to me that you were in peril. They would ride to a rendezvous with the lad, they said, and be back in an hour. They have not done so, and Roger fears they fell into the hands of Sir Nicholas Leslie."

"It is true that they have. I have just received news of it myself. Get the men together that they may start for Damory at once."

Rance obeyed and, once he was outside, Nicholas Leslie came out of the shadow. "Do you doubt my word now?" he asked.

"Nay. What do you want?"

"My vengeance."

"My life?"

"Not here. I am not minded to pay with mine! You surrender to me, rescue or no rescue. Otherwise—well—I hold a Damory, Ruth."

"What proof have I that you will keep your word, cowardly dog that you are?"

"You must take the chance of that," Nicholas sneered. "Well, young upstart, which is it to be, yourself or Ruth?"

"You know the answer to that. Ruth goes free."

"And you surrender, rescue or no rescue, on the famous word of Damory?"

"I do." Rex drew his sword and handed it to Nicholas.

"Put it back," Nicholas ordered. "I do not want any following by that squire of yours. He must think you go willingly."

"That is easily managed." Rex buckled on his sword. "Muffle yourself well, Sir Nicholas. If the men recognize you, no word of mine can save you. Now come."

Followed by his unwelcome visitor, he went outside. Rance was waiting.

"Go to the King, Rance, and tell him what we have heard. Ask his leave to push on at once for Damory. I will ride forth immediately with this messenger. When Mistress Ruth returns, bid her be of good courage and do you serve her loyally."

"But when will you return, Sir Rex?"

"I do not know." Rex mounted his horse. "Farewell, old

friend, until we meet again."

Rance stood looking after them as the two galloped off. "I like it not," he muttered. "It is Sir Rex that Sir Nicholas is after, a murrain on him! Roger shall take the men to Damory and, with three or four, I will follow to see what is in the wind."

Rex and Nicholas Leslie rode rapidly and in silence. Chances of escape, there seemed none. The confident bearing of Nicholas told that his plans were well laid. It was hard to acquiesce in this tame fashion. The very fact of the victory, of restored honors and bright future, had roused all the desire of life again. It was a fiercer fight than that of Bosworth Field that Rex fought with himself as he followed in the direction indicated by his kinsman.

At noontime, Nicholas paused and bade Rex go into a wayside inn and procure provisions for the way. A portion of these they ate hastily while the horses rested. Then they pushed on. The sun went down; the stars came out; and the moon had risen an hour or so before Nicholas paused in a woodland glade.

"We will rest here," he said. "Play me no tricks, my fair kinsman."

"You hold the upper hand at present, Nicholas. You need not fear."

Nicholas scowled. "Do you care for naught?" he snarled. "You go to no easy fate, I warn you."

"The longest day must end at last. You can kill me, Nicholas. Beyond that, you cannot go."

"And you care not?" Nicholas queried, wondering.

"I do not say that."

"Well, rest now. We can waste but little time. I must get back to Devon. Once among mine own rascals, I shall be safe."

Rex obeyed. Lying there under the stars, his thoughts were busy. Where were the maids? What trouble and suffering were about them? Would he see them? His heart beat high with longing for a few brief words of farewell, for the touch of Joyce's hand and the eager love of Ruth's face. He slept at last, but Nicholas roused him at dawn. The journey recommenced, and nightfall found them on the Devon hills. Here Nicholas redoubled his caution. He reconnoitered frequently and listened over and over again for approaching footsteps.

"What do you fear?" asked Rex at last.

"The Torsmen," Nicholas answered briefly. "A murrain upon them! They were put down with fire and sword but they are unbroken still. My life would not be worth an hour's purchase did they guess me close at hand. Only at Castle Leslie shall we be safe from them."

He had spoken true of fire and sword. Blackened walls met their gaze everywhere; desolate farmhouses spoke of a vengeance which had been wreaked on innocent and guilty alike. But the horses were too weary to push on, and Rex showed signs of exhaustion from hard riding with an unhealed wound. Nicholas drew rein near a ruined tower.

"We will wait here," he said. "Castle Leslie is still a good three leagues hence."

They broke their fast, tethered the horses, and then lay down to rest. Nicholas soon slept, but Rex lay wakeful again. A strange journey this was in very truth and the strangest part of it Nicholas Leslie's trust in his word. What had he done with the maids? Rex asked himself again. Suddenly, he turned with the sense of eyes upon him. A malevolent face was peering round the doorway, but as he rose, it vanished and a swift rustle told of hurried flight. Rex bent over Nicholas.

"Up, Nicholas Leslie!" he said. "We have been spied upon and the spy has escaped."

Nicholas was on his feet at once. "It is a ride for life then," he said. "They will be upon us. What? The horses are gone! Then we are lost."

Rex looked at the tower. "The two of us should be able to hold yon stairway," he suggested. "Come quickly."

He ran to the tower with Nicholas at his heels. They reached its shelter none too soon, for a band of men was approaching. Torsmen, fully armed, they were, and marching in a fashion which told of their training years agone in the Leslie ranks. One tall swarthy man was leader, and his quick eyes sighted the fugitives.

"To the tower," he shouted, and with one accord his followers reached the stairs.

But they were nonplussed for the moment. Two men alone could advance, and Rex and Nicholas with drawn swords looked formidable. But they rallied swiftly, and the fight began. It was a fierce one indeed, for the Torsmen were agile and strong, well versed in sword-play, and the duel on the stairs was sharp and fast. But Nicholas, pressed by a wily foe, missed his footing and fell headlong. With a howl of triumph, his foes were upon him, raining blows upon his prostrate form. He must have been instantly killed had it not been that in their fury, they hampered each other. Rex cleared the stairs at a bound. His sword flashed left and right and his unexpected onrush made them give way. He dragged Nicholas within the stairway, and, standing above him, renewed the unequal fight. It must end in his defeat at last. One man, single-handed, could not hold a mob at bay indefinitely. But help was at hand. A clatter of horsehoofs sounded and then a clear voice called a familiar war cry, "Damory, Damory, fight for our young lord's sake!"

Rance and half a dozen men-at-arms, all well mounted, appeared on the scene. The Torsmen, bewildered by this new attack, gathered up their wounded and fled, Rance not troubling to follow but making for Rex's side.

"How came you here, Rance?"

"I disobeyed you and methinks that it was well that I did,

Sir Rex. What mad plan have you afoot? Who is this? Nicholas Leslie?"

The squire's hand tightened on his dagger, but Rex knocked it aside.

"Not on an unconscious and wounded man, Rance. Touch him not."

"He would slay you without a moment's hesitation," Rance growled. "Well, have your way, Sir Rex. My advice is to leave him here. He looks as if he were wounded unto death and a good thing if he is. But I suppose you will tend him."

Rex smiled, as he knelt down and began to staunch the wounds. Nicholas twisted and moaned with pain, but he seemed unable to recognize anyone. Rex looked at him and then turned to his men.

"Make a litter," he ordered. "Rance, we must ride for Castle Leslie. Do you know the way? The maids are there held prisoners."

"Many a time and oft have I ridden it with your father, Sir Rex. Where is your horse?"

"Stolen, I fear, but I see you have a led one. We must go at a footpace because of Nicholas Leslie."

"Good riddance indeed if he dies on the road," Rance muttered. But he lifted the fallen foe gently enough when it came to the moment of placing him in the hastily constructed litter.

It was a tedious ride. The moon had waned; the way was rough and, as Rex had said, more than a walk was impossible on account of the wounded man. The dawn had broken when they came in sight of Castle Leslie, a picturesque pile of gray stone buildings dating from Norman days. Rex rode forward waving a white kerchief, and a man-at-arms came out to meet him. He recognized Thorsby.

"Your lord is sorely wounded, Thorsby," Rex called. "The Torsmen set upon us and but for help of my own men who followed us we had both been slain. Let us in and send someone for the nearest leech, for Sir Nicholas needs more skilled aid than yours or mine."

The man hesitated a moment, but a look at his wounded master decided him, and he lowered the drawbridge himself. Sir Nicholas was lifted out and borne to his own chamber. Thorsby spoke gruffly.

"Do you come as friend or foe, my lord of Damory?"

"As prisoner of your lord, rescue or no rescue," Rex answered.

"'Troth, you will not be that long," Rance growled.

"Rance, you and the men may bide with me for the nonce," Rex told him sternly. "But you must hold yourself as guests of Castle Leslie. I shall need you for a guard to Mistress Ruth. We come peaceably, Thorsby, and I vouch for my men here, if they be not attacked. Is Mistress Ruth here? And Mistress Joyce?"

"Rex, O Rex." Joyce herself came running down the stairs followed by Ruth. "Has he got you as he said? Oh, why did you come with him?"

"Life and honors are barren things without you and Ruth, Joyce." Rex held out his hand to her, while his arm stole about his sister. "How did you both come here?"

"Sir Nicholas Leslie tricked us. A man, riding up, who bore Damory's badge, told us that the battle was lost and that you were in peril. We must follow him. We did so and were carried off. Then, we were told that we were hostages for you, and Sir Nicholas boasted that he would have his vengeance."

"He is sore wounded now."

"Then we can leave him to his men and go back to Damory."

"I cannot. I am prisoner, rescue or no rescue. Moreover, these rough men-at-arms cannot tend him properly. I must care for him."

Ruth tossed her red-gold head. "You are a knight errant in very truth, Rex. Have you no sense? Why nurse your foe back to life that he may take yours?"

"Because he is wounded and alone and our mother's kinsman, Ruth."

"This is simply troubadour folly, Rex. But if you insist on
biding here, so do I."

"I will not send you away yet, sister mine. Now I must go."

"I will go with you, Rex. You cannot manage alone," said
Joyce. "I will go to nurse him, though, father of mine as he is, I
would as soon tend a snake."

"Then, Rance, look you to Mistress Ruth," Rex said. "Thorsby
is coming. What news of your master?"

"He lies at death's door, Sir Rex, so says the leech. He must
have skillful tendance, and we have no one here."

"Send to Damory for Nurse Gillian," Rex proposed. "Mistress
Joyce and I will care for him with her help. We will go to him
now."

"I shall take my share," Ruth insisted. "I be not Messere Saint
George in person as you are, Rex, but I will not leave you alone."

A strange life commenced for them all. Nurse Gillian, once
installed, sent most of the nurses to the right-about except Rex
and Joyce. Ruth had started to take her share, but her presence
seemed to excite the invalid, and she devoted herself to the
ill-assorted household, for on one side were Rance and his men
augmented by more from Damory, and on the other, Thorsby
and the band of Devonshire soldiery.

"How you do it, Ruth, is a mystery to me," Rex commented
one day. "Methought we should have civil war on our hands
before three days had sped, yet somehow you have welded these
rough men together."

"They admire you, Rex. Thorsby told me he never heard of
such a fight as you waged with the Torsmen when Sir Nicholas
was wounded. I made Rance come and describe it. They were
friends afterwards."

"*Maiden's hand brings harmony and joy and peace to Damory,*" Rex quoted, but Ruth's face grew white.

"Quote not the old punishment, Rex. There is one part unfulfilled. Would that Damory's lord had conquered Damory's foe! My heart misgives me for your safety, Rex. Must you stay?"

"I gave my word, Ruth. Fear not, is not God caring for us?"

"I know. I can trust for myself but it is hard to do so for another, Rex. Joyce is braver, but I see no way out."

"We do not have to see it," Rex said thoughtfully. "So often in this strife the future has been dark. Even death is not the worst that can befall. Nicholas with his stained honor is more to be pitied. His ravings have made one think of a soul punished."

"Is he better?"

"I think so. At least Nurse Gillian thinks his danger is past. The leech has not come yet. I must go back and relieve Joyce."

He left her and returned to the sick chamber. Nicholas was silent but fully conscious at last. Joyce slipped away, and Rex took her place as the old leech came in. He made a careful examination of the fast healing wounds.

"You are doing well, Sir Nicholas. It has been a narrow escape for you, but there are not many who have had kinsfolk to give such skilled and devoted care as you have had."

He bustled away, not heeding Nicholas Leslie's embarrassed thanks. Rex sat down beside the bed and sat there quietly, aware that Nicholas was staring at him in odd fashion.

"What did you save me for?" he asked abruptly. "Why did you not leave me where I fell? Did you think that I would be weakling enough to forgive?"

"I had no thought of that, Sir Nicholas. No one but a cowardly dog would leave a wounded man helpless at the mercy of his foes."

"Why did you not go when you had found the maids?"

"I had passed my word to you."

"You ever play the fool in regard to your plighted word, Rex Damory."

Nicholas relapsed into silence again, but in the days of tedious convalescence, he watched his kinsman narrowly. To Joyce, he showed no gratitude and delighted in demanding her services, watching with malicious pleasure her efforts to overcome her distaste for her task.

"A loyal daughter," he would comment mockingly. "It is well that I have so loving a heart at my service for my declining years."

"Ruth, do you think he will make me go with him?" Joyce said to her friend. "What shall I do?"

"Wait till he is stronger and give him your opinion of him," Ruth advised fierily. "The King is your friend, and you have an assured place at court. Prithee, do not turn into a second Messere Saint George. Surely, Rex is enough."

"I am ashamed of myself when I see how patient Rex is."

"What is puzzling me is how we are to rescue Rex," Ruth said. "It is like Sir Nicholas to have tricked him with that rescue or no rescue. But he shall not have Rex, even if I have to bring the whole Royal Force down on Castle Leslie."

As Nicholas grew stronger, the situation became more tense. Rex made a fresh effort to send the girls back to Damory but found himself worsted in wordy combat. Ruth refused point-blank to go, and Joyce followed her lead. Rex decided that an appeal for them must be made to Nicholas himself. In the meantime, Ruth had laid her plans and despatched a messenger to London.

Nicholas broached the subject first. Rex came into the room to find him in the great chair, wearied with the exertion that he had made to walk on the battlement.

"Where have you been?" Nicholas demanded.

"With Joyce."

"You follow her still?"

"I do. To tell you the truth, Sir Nicholas, were I not in the shadow of death, my dreams would take another turn. In days to come, I, too, would bring a Leslie bride to Damory."

"You would wed with *my* maid? Methought the unsullied honor of the Damorys would scorn alliance with me."

"Joyce outweighs all else."

"A paragon in truth, with as mad a sense of honor as your own. You would be well matched. How the proud girl hates her ancestry!"

"She has done her duty well. You could scarcely expect her love under the circumstances."

Nicholas yawned. "Methinks I paid her out in any cast. Faith, but her face when I claimed her atoned for much!" He laughed harshly. "And the King did not even investigate my proof."

"Do you mean to say that you had none?"

Nicholas laughed again. "None but my word which, as you reminded me not so long ago, counts for naught."

"You coward!" Rex clutched Nicholas in anger and the wounded man shrank back before his blazing eyes. "You have lied to Joyce and tormented her all these months? You would take this vengeance on a maid, you cowardly dog?"

Nicholas wriggled himself free. "Sir Galahad is roused at last. I have found out how to anger *you*, Rex Damory."

"You have." Rex bit his lip, fighting for self-control. "Is this another of your lies?"

"I speak the truth for once, my fair kinsman. You need never have believed me. The priest at the village church will tell you all that you want to know. Jack Deventry, Joyce's father, did great service to mine, and I befriended her."

"If you can call it that."

"She was homeless. Well, best go a-wooing, my young springald."

"I stand in the shadow of death." Rex spoke gravely now. "I have no right to bring a cloud on any maid."

"Do you not realize that you and Ruth have won these rascals of mine? Not one of them will touch you, Rex Damory."

"Your own hand will soon be strong enough for a death blow."

"And you are not going to appeal to your Red Rose King?"

"The bargain was made, and I accepted it. I should not have nursed you back to health to die upon a scaffold."

"I should have done it in your place."

"Well, we be enemies. If you owe me aught, I would ask that my death end the feud. War not on Ruth."

Nicholas smiled grimly. "I have no mind to meddle with fire, good cousin. Ruth is best left alone. I do not often own that I have met my match but I assuredly did there. Troth what a tongue the maid has! She spoiled my long-laid scheme of vengeance. I meant Hugh Damory's maid to bring about his death and yours. But Ruth, for all her hate of Red Rose rebels, will have naught of crooked ways. Lie she will not. She has all the daring of the Damorys too. All England will be about my ears if I harm you."

"I think that she will respect my wishes, Sir Nicholas."

"Little you know her! You cannot manage Ruth. But a truce to this. A murrain on you, my hands are bound. You know I cannot take your life under these circumstances. Go seek your maid and get you both to Damory."

"And Joyce?"

"Win her if you can, my paladin. I balk you not."

"There is your own safety to be considered, Sir Nicholas. You should go overseas at once. The royal forces may reach Devonshire at any time now."

"You should have been a monk, Rex Damory, you play the saint so well. Send FitzAllen to me; he will see me safe."

Marvelling at this strange change in affairs, Rex sought for Joyce and Ruth. He found them together, planning, as usual, ways and means out of their difficulties. Ruth sprang up joyously as she caught sight of his face.

"Rex, Rex, you bring good news!"

"Nicholas Leslie has given me back my promise."

"Your patience has won him at last," Joyce cried.

Rex laughed. "I fear not. I rather think it is because I lost my temper with him just now. He has the most marvellous respect for yours, Ruth. But I bear other tidings which will bring joy to you, Joyce *Deventry*."

"Why do you call me that?"

"Because you *are* Joyce Deventry. Nicholas owned to me just now that he lied as usual. His maid died in the great fever. You are no kin to him."

The color flashed into Joyce's face. She clasped her hands nervously. "Rex, is it really true? Do you think he speaks truth at last?" she asked.

"Naught but the truth, ungrateful child." The jeering voice came from the door, and they turned to face Nicholas. "I was minded to drag you with me to comfort mine old age, but what could I do with a puling maid overseas? Well, Ruth Damory, have you no word for me? I have let your Sir Galahad go, although I well-nigh got him hanged for the murder of the verderer in Epping."

"You coward, was that your plan?" Ruth clenched her hands fiercely. "I have thanked the Torsmen who burned Leslie Tower in my mind many a time for frustrating your evil plots. Methinks it had been well if they had finished their work the other day."

Nicholas laughed mockingly. "You thought this spitfire would respect your wishes, Rex Damory. Do you really think that your death would end the feud? Well, well, you all have tricked me, but I have had a vengeance, nevertheless. Damory's lord for four long years has known no happy day."

"You are wrong there, Sir Nicholas. I have had many," Rex said.

"You are not Damory's lord." Nicholas laughed loud and long. "Aye, FitzAllen, bring the prisoner in and let them see what has been worse than death."

He stood aside and they all stared. A man entered, haggard and emaciated, with ragged garments thick with mildew from the dankness of a dungeon. "What do you want, Nicholas Leslie?" he asked and, as he spoke, Rex sprang forward, while Rance, pushing FitzAllen aside, caught the prisoner's hand in his, raining passionate kisses upon it.

"My lord, my lord, my own dear lord, Sir Hugh," he sobbed.

"Father!" Rex flung his arms about him in unbelievable joy.

"My lad, my lad." Sir Hugh held him close. "Rex, Rex, are you in his power too?"

"Nay, he goes free, a plague upon him. He has outwitted me at every turn. But I am not minded to be cheated of everything." Nicholas Leslie clenched his hands. "You are safe, Hugh Damory, while life was not worth the living; now that it is sweet again, you pay. Hold back the squire, Rance, Forrest; pull Rex Damory aside, Tyrrell; Thorsby, stab the prisoner to the heart!"

Forrest sprang on Rance and bore him to the ground; two others seized Rex and held him fast in spite of his struggles; Thorsby drew his dagger. But before he could do more, Ruth flung herself between. A distant bugle call sounded on the air.

"Put up that dagger, Thorsby," she commanded. "Nicholas Leslie, I had word that the royal troops will be here today. That bugle call is theirs. If you and your men value your worthless lives, get you gone."

"Out of the way, Ruth Damory, or by my faith, you share your mother's fate," Nicholas ordered. "Strike on, rascal."

But Thorsby sheathed his weapon. "Mistress Ruth is safe from me, Sir Nicholas. She has stood between us and Damory's men too many times for us to harm her. Aye, if she wants this prisoner, she shall have him."

Rance had wrenched himself free and was shouting loudly for his men. Tyrrell and his companion loosed their hold on Rex. With drawn weapons, the men of Damory entered and drew around their lord.

"Shall we cut the miscreant down?" Rance cried, as he held his weapon at Nicholas Leslie's heart.

"Nay." Ruth spoke clearly. "Let him go. Stand close about Sir Hugh and Rex, come hither to me. Nicholas Leslie, get you gone!"

The baffled man glared upon her. "Come, Forrest; come, Tyrrell; and let the King hang the rest if he chooses," Nicholas ordered. "You have won, Rex Damory, thanks to this shrew."

With head held high, he walked out, and presently they heard the clatter of horses' hoofs across the drawbridge.

Sir Hugh had sunk down into a chair as the armed men drew away from him. He held out shaking hands. "It is Ruth, my maid, my little maid?" he asked.

"Your maid, Father." Ruth flung eager arms about him while Rex knelt at his side.

"But how came you here?" Rex asked. "We have mourned you as dead these four years past."

"I stood on the very threshold of death, lad. It was on the scaffold that Nicholas stayed the executioner and brought me by night to a dungeon here." He shivered a little. "There were hard days, Rex, days which will not bear repeating. Nicholas came to torment me from time to time. He told me you were disgraced; that you were dead. Never once would he tell me of my maid here. But what has happened and who is this?" He pointed to Joyce.

"Joyce Deventry, homeless now save for us."

"Jack Deventry's maid? She will not be homeless while we live." Sir Hugh smiled at her. "You said royal troops were coming, Ruth? I do not understand."

"The Wars of the Roses are ended and the Red Rose rules again," Rex said. "Henry of Richmond is England's King and he weds the little White Rose Princess that Ruth and Joyce and I love so well. It is a new England, Father, and Damory's feud is done, thanks to Ruth here. *Maiden's hand brings harmony and joy and peace to Damory.*"

"And methinks the punishment is lifted." Joyce looked from Sir Hugh to Rex, from the young man's scarred hands to the old one's haggard face. "It is all fulfilled now, Rex. *Damory's lord in bitter woe, has conquered Damory's fiercest foe.*"

XI

Postscript

MY STORY is placed in the period of the Wars of the Roses which extends from the last year of the reign of Edward IV to the beginning of the reign of Henry VII. This war which devastated England for three generations had a respite from open warfare from the battle of Tewkesbury in 1471 to the battle of Bosworth Field in 1485.

King Edward IV, like many of his race, proved to be a good ruler, and it was not until the news of his ill health became public that plots and counterplots on behalf of the Red Rose began to be ominous. Such as remained of the great Lancastrian lords had taken refuge in France and chiefly at the court of Brittany, but there were left in England many of the lesser nobles who lived in retirement upon their estates and who were rather closely watched by the victorious Yorkists.

The imminent death of the king and a child heir revived the hopes of these nobles, and plots were discovered from time to time, mostly in connection with an effort to bring the young

Earl of Richmond to the head of his party. For this reason King Edward made a definite effort to get him into his hands, an effort which Richard the Third repeated a little later.

The poverty and distress which followed on the Wars engendered much discontent among the peasantry, particularly in the south, and riots and uprisings were more or less frequent and were put down with a stern hand. For the purposes of the story I have availed myself of these two conditions without, however, taking any particular plot or rising as the basis. What I have tried to do is to make a picture of the conditions which would surround a Red Rose lad who had fallen into captivity to the house of York.

At the court, strife was still more acute. The marriage of the king to Lady Elizabeth Woodville, the widow of a Lancastrian knight, had been very unpopular with the Yorkist nobles. The king favored her brothers, Lords Grey and Rivers, and placed them in positions of importance, while the kinsmen of her first husband found places about the court.

The chief opponent of the Queen and her party was the king's youngest brother, Richard, Duke of Gloucester. Concerning him there are many contradictory opinions, but the truth probably lies between them all. He was a true Plantagenet type, ruthless and ambitious, with a power of intrigue which few of his race equalled. He was a powerful prince with strong friends, and no one seems to have dared during his brother's lifetime to have done more than whisper that he was anything but loyal to his brother's family. He was present at Tewkesbury when young Prince Edward of Lancaster died and in the Tower on the night of the passing of Henry the Sixth. There were ugly stories which connected him definitely with the death of his elder brother, George of Clarence, but all these were vigorously denied at the court.

Doubtless he was plotting for the throne and some apprehension seems to have been entertained for the young heir, for King Edward only allowed his eldest son to be in London for short intervals, believing him to be safer when separated from his brother. Richard probably thought that Parliament would exercise its ancient right and pass over a child, but when he found this was not the case, he started on the ruthless system he had employed before of removing obstacles from his path. By this, although he obtained his desire, he aroused such hatred and opposition that his brief reign of two years was one of continual turmoil.

It is this view of his character that I have tried to portray using Shakespeare's picture of him as giving the Tudor view of this last king of the house of York. The major characters of the story are not historical nor have I attempted to identify them with any historical place or personage. Damory Court was near Blandford but of what part it actually played in the Wars of the Roses I have found no record and therefore, because the surroundings are familiar to me, I have made it the home place of Damory's lord.

The Leslies are likewise imaginary and are based upon the fact that, owing to the friendship between Henry V and the captive King James of Scotland, some of the Scottish followers of the royal prisoner settled in England and married English brides.

In two minor points, the story is not capable of historical proof. There is no actual evidence that Richard the Third was in the Tower on the night of the murder of the Princes (the actual date of the murder is in doubt), and it was given out that he was at Warwick, but he frequently employed incognito, and so it was not impossible for him to be there. The stories of the topography of Bosworth Field are contradictory, and in my description of the battle, I have again resorted to Shakespeare.

My desire is that the readers of this book will find in it a picture of a time which was critical in that it was the end of the Old and the beginning of a New England, a period full of color and human interest, which is often misunderstood because of its confusion and the similarity of names. I hope that each one will see that the boys and girls of those troublous times were indeed boys and girls like themselves, who solved their difficulties by courage, faith, and loyalty.